WORDS FROM
THE COUNTRYMAN

'Makes one feel in the country'
Thomas Hardy

The Countryman

comes from the country

AUTUMN 1959   Volume 56   No 3

Open to Visitors   *The Marquess of Hertford*

Our Hunting Monkey   *Vera Ryder*

North Across New England   *Francis Russell*

Painters and Place   *John Dalton*

SHEEP STREET   BURFORD   OXFORDSHIRE

THREE SHILLINGS QUARTERLY

In 1959 the familiar dark green cover of The Countryman *was illustrated for the first time, with a series in that year by John Nash, R.A. For the autumn issue, he produced a richly evocative orchard scene.*

WORDS FROM
THE COUNTRYMAN

'Makes one feel in the country' **Thomas Hardy**

Edited by VALERIE PORTER

David and Charles

TITLE PAGE:

Wood engraving by Christopher Wormell, commissioned by The Countryman
as a special limited edition print for its 75th birthday.

A DAVID & CHARLES BOOK

Copyright © David & Charles Limited 2007

David & Charles is an F+W Publications Inc. company
4700 East Galbraith Road
Cincinnati, OH 45236

First published in the UK in 2007

Text copyright © the contributors or *The Countryman* 2007
Illustrations copyright © the contributors or *The Countryman* 2007
Text and illustrations originally appeared in *The Countryman* 1927-2007
Introductory text and editorial notes copyright © Valerie Porter 2007

ISBN-13: 978-0-7153-2704-3
ISBN-10: 0-7153-2704-6

Printed in Finland by WS Bookwell
for David & Charles
Brunel House, Newton Abbot, Devon

Commissioning Editor: Jane Trollope
Editor: Emily Pitcher
Desk Editor: Demelza Hookway
Project Editor: James Loader
Layout: Sue Cleave
Production Controller: Ros Napper

Visit our website at www.davidandcharles.co.uk

David & Charles books are available from all good bookshops; alternatively you
can contact our Orderline on 0870 9908222 or write to us at FREEPOST EX2
110, D&C Direct, Newton Abbot, TQ12 4ZZ (no stamp required UK only);
US customers call 800-289-0963 and Canadian customers call 800-840-5220.

Contents

6
Introduction

8
1 The Pioneer Years
1927–1937

34
2 The Challenges of War
1938–1946

68
3 Rebuilding the Countryside
1947–1957

100
4 Prosperity and Optimism
1958–1967

125
5 Agribusiness Versus the Home Acre
1968–1977

151
6 Urban Migrants
1978–1989

182
7 In Our Time
1990–2007

Index 219
Credits & Acknowledgments 224

Introduction

THE COUNTRYMAN has always reflected what is happening in the countryside – the good and the bad, the nostalgic and the current, as well as glimpses into the future, embracing a wide range of social strata and attitudes – and it is a wonderful source of social history, full of nuggets of curious information that bring different periods to life. Over its first 80 years some subjects have been debated or described time and time again, especially fox-hunting, bee-keeping, glow-worms, nightjars, rook gatherings, screaming frogs, dealing with moles, birds of prey, rat swarms, hedgehogs, the antics of blackbirds, the habits of livestock, numerous stories of cats and dogs, weather extremes, walking at night, light pollution, tramps and gypsies, scarecrows, follies and defensive pillboxes, as well as pithy comments on whatever political party might be in power at the time.

The character of *The Countryman* was firmly established right from the start by its extraordinary and dominating 'Founder Editor', John W. Robertson Scott. A tall, spare and elegantly dressed man with an instantly recognizable Shavian beard and thick head of hair (both already white by the time he founded the magazine in 1927), Robertson Scott kept firm editorial control on every word that was published in his quarterly review, whether the writers were merely his

The always immaculate Founder Editor, J.W. Robertson Scott, photographed at Idbury Manor on the eve of his 90th birthday in April 1956.

readers or were some of the most famous or socially high-born in the land. He cultivated the names of his day assiduously and elicited articles from several prime ministers and other leading politicians as well as numerous titled and usually landed gentry.

He frequently reproduced their hand-written signatures and even hand-written letters.

Robertson Scott was well aware that his new review needed solid financial backing and he travelled regularly to London from his Cotswolds home at Idbury to persuade advertisers to take up space in the journal. But not just any advertisers: he had strong ideas on the type of product or service that should be given the honour of access to his largely upper-middle-class readership, and frequently rejected approaches by those he thought unsuitable. He was a man of principle and strongly held views; he was a vegetarian, a 'naturist', a lover of the classics fond of quoting the likes of Virgil and Cicero; he disliked hunting and shooting, loved dogs and cats, and had a burning desire to 'improve' the lot of those who lived in rural areas.

After 21 years Robertson Scott was succeeded by a series of long-serving editors. In the past decade the changes in editor have been more frequent, but for the most part the magazine has maintained a non-party political stance and a mixture of hard fact, tradition, imagination, influence, intelligent observation and comment, stinging criticism, quirkiness and wry humour. At its best it continues to campaign for a better countryside and a better life for those who live in and visit rural Britain, while at the same time lifting the spirit, broadening knowledge of the living world, and entertaining with wit, self-deprecation and story-telling.

VALERIE PORTER
Milland, Summer 2007

1927-1937

The Pioneer Years

W hen *The Countryman* was born in 1927, a year after the General Strike, Stanley Baldwin was Prime Minister and the countryside was sliding rapidly into an agricultural depression. Conditions for country workers were not good, but those who worked on the land and in the villages were finding a new voice: old class divisions were at last being broken and people had the courage to complain about low wages and often atrocious rural housing. In addition, 'Rural', with a capital R, was coming into fashion: the middle classes were spreading into the countryside – as ramblers and cyclists, as motorists out for a Sunday drive, as commuters and as owners of weekend cottages (they could buy a good one for £200–£400) – and many of them chatted over their dinner tables about the need for 'Rural Improvement'. Launching his new quarterly review 'from the country' at his home at Idbury Manor, J.W. Robertson Scott, already 60 years old, remarked that more thought than ever before was being given to 'Rural Problems'. He stated that his aim was to make 'Rural Life what it ought to be, and can be, *within our time*' and he believed that thousands felt deeply 'how much is *within our reach* for Rural Civilisation'. It is easy to mock what today might

(Above) Always with an eye for promoting his magazine, J.W.R.S. produced a flyer in 1929 including this illustration, captioned: '"The Countryman" Editorial and Publishing Office in the Country, which is why it is a really rural periodical.'

sound pretentious and patronising, but the earnest do-gooders were above all well meaning and, in the end, they did make a difference.

In the countryside, the first signs of a major revolution in farming practice were in sight: those of mechanisation, and what would in due course be the replacement of living horsepower by the horsepower of the tractor and other fossil-fuel-driven machinery. But in the 1930s the impact of the tractor was still tentative. It would take a world war to displace the horse.

The editor throughout these 'pioneer years' was, of course, J.W. Robertson Scott himself: a man with a vast network of contacts and with many friends in high places, able to summon articles and thoughts from some of the most influential in the land. He proudly boasted on the front cover of the first issue (April, 1927) that contributors included a string of lords, knights and government ministers. An accomplished name dropper, he littered the pages of his new quarterly review with mentions of those he knew in politics, in high society, and in the world of literature.

Several regular features were established in these early years. Among them, the initially anonymous 'Diary of a Fruit Farmer' (later 'Fruit Grower') became a firm favourite over many years: the author was in due course revealed to be Raymond Bush, who eventually emigrated to Jamaica but who, in the meantime, was a humorous teller of tiny anecdotes, many of them absolutely nothing to do with his considerable expertise in growing fruit, and usually published several months after the actual diary dates. Anonymity and pseudonyms were widely used by regular contributors, such as 'Student' (writing on agriculture), 'Salfario' (angling), 'Innkeeper's Daughter' (country cooking) and Solomon Wiseacre (or that may have been his real name – he wrote from his 'old homestead'). Very often, frustratingly, authors and advisers were identified only by initials.

Another favourite series was 'The Country House Aeroplane', which certainly gave a flavour of the period: many readers, it seems, were wealthy enough to own a light plane and had space in which it could take off and land. This touch of the upper class in the countryside comes through quite strongly, with articles and letters from assorted landed gentry, the upper middle class, the military and old colonials. Domestic staff were taken for granted, even if only a gardener and a cook or maid.

'Countryman Club' gave readers a chance to tell their own stories and sometimes to ask for help from other readers. It was actually a cunning way of encouraging readers to build a sense of loyalty with 'their' quarterly magazine, by joining a 'club'. This feeling of belonging was also apparent in 'Readers' Motoring Tales' and in the long-running 'Tail Corn' series in which readers could win a guinea for the best snippet of vernacular or rustic humour, though one has the impression that the 'rustics' were probably turning it on for the condescending listeners who found their speech so 'quaint'.

Other regular features of the period had titles such as 'Why I live in the country', 'Cheaper to live in the country' (or not), 'My garden' (by various famous people, including a prime minister) and a nice little technical series on gramophones and wirelesses and, eventually, rural television sets. There was also a series about different 'rural authors' – several of whom were regular contributors – and diaries from farmers large and small, often with little experience at first, which gave a lot of down-to-earth information about the problems and joys of farming. Agriculture was treated very seriously in these inter-war years and there were many lengthy articles on the subject.

Major topics in this first decade of *The Countryman* ranged from flying to nudism, embracing along the way subjects such as vegetarians, electricity for villages, wheatmeal bread, river swimming, fox-hunting (generally against), improvement of cottages, tramps (a recurring fascination over several decades of *The Countryman* along with gypsies), enterprises for ex-servicemen or retired city men wishing to make a living in the country (particularly fruit farming and bee-keeping), the inappropriateness of marble in rural graveyards, the cleverness of dogs, and frequent observations on massed starlings and on the virtues of queen wasps. There is much input from the readers themselves – which is an economical way of acquiring material for any publication, and also gives a wonderfully broad range of experiences, knowledge and imagination.

But much more of the material came from the editor himself, in lengthy columns such as 'As One Countryman to Another', 'In the Country and Out of It' and 'As It Seems to Some of Us', and he often 'signed' them with his name written cryptically in Pitman's shorthand.

In its first decade, the young journal was bursting with zeal, enthusiasm and ideas, and it gradually expanded from the original 'pocket-size' 96 pages to a peak of 432 pages each issue by 1937. Yet it still maintained its price at half-a-crown (two shillings and sixpence, or 12½p). To everyone's surprise except the founder-editor's, sales had reached 13,000 copies. The next decade, which included the war years, would see a dramatic rise to 55,000 copies printed for each issue.

1927

As It Was

BY A NONAGENARIAN

'Could my mother give Mrs. Hinks some newspapers to wrap her baby in', is one of my earliest rural recollections of things heard in the big house in which my girlhood was spent.

The wretched people in the cottages reproduced themselves like rabbits. As one poor woman told me, when I grew up, and was married, 'Our bit of love, 'tis our only tenderness.'

One must be plain about the conditions that existed, for the books are mealy-mouthed. It was significant that in one village there was – as in many another village, alas! – a row of cottage slums called 'The Pest Houses.' Cottages with such a name had memories, but in our day it was a common thing for four cottages to have one horror of a privy among them.

Far out in the fields on our estate, a labourer lived with his daughter. We were told one day that there was a baby there. No doubt existed that the girl's parent was the father. Such a beautiful creature that girl was!

Another woman, as she told me of an unwanted baby that her husband and she were adding to their dreary home, told me that its coming was 'God's will.' Outside the cottage there was a calf with five legs. I asked the woman if the five legs were 'God's will.' Later on I had the ghastly news that her child had been born with some redundant member.

… In those days there were man-traps in the hedges, orchards and plantations. We sometimes used to think that there were labourers who came to regard their daughters as a source of income by being a species of man-trap. The girls who were sent up to service to London and into the towns seemed many of them to be seduced as a matter of course, and the grand-parents did not do so badly by keeping the base-borns. But farmers also had their share in the seduction of labourers' daughters.

I go back to these sorry things of the past by way of encouragement to you. As a woman of 93, I have lived to see a revolution in thought and feeling, as well as in material things. When your younger readers know what has been achieved within one old woman's recollections, they may be hopeful of the future for which they are working.

[Editor's note: 'Nonagenarian' was Mrs. H.B. Taylor, of Cheyne Walk, who died aged 94 in 1929. V.L.P.]

Three Premiers and the Land

The straw in Palmerston's mouth was legendary, but Mr. Baldwin's pigs are real. The Premier actually has pigs, good pigs, and is, I know for a fact, keen about them.

Although in his boyhood Mr. Ramsay MacDonald dug 'taties', and speaks with feeling and conviction on his party's policy for agriculture, it is impossible to claim him as a cultivator of the land, past or present. Even an orchard, on his quarter of an acre at Lossiemouth would be, as he once said to me, 'a sorry affair; I can run to whin bushes that produce to my mind and eye the golden fruit of blossom, but to my body no fruit at all'. Attached to his house in Hampstead, Mr. MacDonald has a small garden in which he sometimes potters. An outstanding distinction of the ex-Premier-ex-Foreign Minister is, as we know, that he has seen more foreign countries and therefore more of their countrysides than any of his predecessors.

As for Mr. Lloyd George, I must be the only person, I think, who has come on an ex-Premier suffering from stings as a result of a too impetuous sickle attack on nettles. The next day the ardour of this small-holder led him to embark on a campaign with ferrets against the rats which desired to live with his pigs and ducks. The thing that Mr. Lloyd George seemed proudest of was a fine clump of rasps, a variety named after their possessor by the raiser. 'L.G.' is an Alderman of the Surrey County Council, and a shareholder in the Banbury Farmers' Auction Mart.

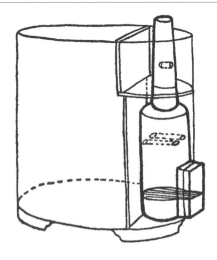

A wooden Japanese-style bath, highly recommended by Robertson Scott, who wrote: 'I have often regretted that no one has tried the experiment of introducing to some more than ordinarily enlightened cottager the inexpensive bath of the Japanese peasant. The diagram sufficiently explains the wooden bath, the cast-iron stove, the fire-bars and the draught slides. The water fills the place where the stove is as well as the bath proper; the wooden division is merely to keep the bather's body from touching the stove. The exceedingly cheap bath illustrated is just large enough to sit in with one's knees to one's chin.'

TI IROUGH PARAGUAYAN SPECTACLES

– COLONIA, COSME, *via* CAAZAPA, PARAGUAY.

You MAY LIKE to hear how England struck me after being here. It is the absence of communal social life. I often visited a beautiful little place with an ancient church. A buxom young woman who owned the old inn told me that they had about two social events per annum. We used to have here two a week, although only, in all, 80 adults. Sunday programmes were got up by nearly every adult running one in turn. We worked harder, lived harder, and were, apart from the possession of a lot of virgin land and forest, poorer than your English peasants. Also, as a crowd, we were neither gifted nor accomplished. But all crowds have gifts when you dig into them. In some English villages nobody seems to dig. What we called our 'social life' was one hundred per cent successful, however much we may have failed otherwise!

1928

LONDON OR THE COUNTRY FOR BRAIN WORK?

'In order to live your life well, play in the country, but work in the town. It is in the great vitality of the great town's life that the individual is stimulated and compelled to think.'

It seemed well worth while to have some informed comment on this expression of opinion by the headmaster of Westminster School. *The Countryman* accordingly communicated with a number of distinguished men and women, and, thanks to their kindness, is able to publish the following statements. The question was, Did they think that their best work was done in the town or in the country?

… THE RIGHT HON. J. RAMSAY MACDONALD. – My experience is not quite that of the Headmaster of Westminster. If I had to choose between the town and the country as a place for working I should unhesitatingly say that I can not only produce more in the latter but that the quality of the work is much better. I think, however, the real fact is that a change from one to the other is necessary, as one's mind requires the rest that comes from variety. To do all your play in the country and all your work in the town seems to me to be a bad rule.

" Higgler: Awlright, bob a pahnd. – Wholesaler: *Good lot this mornin', eighteenpence a pound, rough plucked. Shall I send 'em along? Righto!* – Retailer: *Yes, sir, we shall deliver in half an hour. Two shillings a pound to-day, sir. –* Hotel Superbe: *Volaille de poulet rôti, 5s. 6d. "*

As It Seems to Some of Us
TOWN OR COUNTRY

One of the ex-Premier contributions to the discussion in our April issue, on 'Town or Country for Brain Work', which attracted so much attention, was unfortunately too late with his communication for it to appear in that number, so we have the pleasure of publishing it now:

It is, in my experience (Mr. Lloyd George is kind enough to tell us) the country which stimulates clear thinking and renewed effort. The strain of the town exhausts mind and body. The vitality of the countryside restores them. It is my hope to see the day when all the people of this land will be able to enjoy easy access to the fields and the countryside, and far more of them will find there a happy and a prosperous livelihood. In this era of swift transport and fertile invention it should be within the power of statesmanship to bridge the gulf between town and country, and to enable everyone to gain the stimulus and social amenities of the city, the health and recreation of quiet open spaces.

As we are not without censorious correspondents it may be just as well to mention, perhaps, that faithful to our non-Party attitude, we asked by the same post for the views of Mr. Baldwin, Lord Balfour, Mr. Ramsay MacDonald, and Mr. Lloyd George. Lord Balfour was ill, Mr. Baldwin kindly explained his decision to refrain from Press communications, and so Mr. MacDonald appeared alone. In applying to a few other Members of Parliament of different Parties who have done literary work we were equally blind to Party labels. As it happened, Lord Olivier and Mr. Sidney Webb alone replied.

1929

Other Peoples' Countrysides

Aleppo

Everywhere that Mary went the lamb was sure to go. But Mary had no notion of making the most of her pet. Whereas an inhabitant of Aleppo, according to Mr. M.H. Ellis, in 'Express to Hindustan', 'takes his pet lamb and dyes its fat tail magenta and its ears green or paints a crimson band round its heart or gives it an orange muzzle, after which it is deemed fit to mingle (on the end of a lead) with the gay human medley in the streets. Every afternoon you may see fifty inhabitants strolling with their muttons.'

WHO is the author of the following? – 'Give me the hill road, the bleating of sheep, the clouds, the sun and the rain, the graves of dead races, the thatched roofs of living ones, a pipe and a fire when the day is closing, and a clean bed to lie upon until the sun calls in the morning. If friends fail, the hill road never does. There is nothing in faithfulness like to it, and blessed is the man who has found it.' The new Prime Minister *[Ramsay MacDonald]*.

" *'The old gardener died last night,' writes a reader. 'In the midst of his fearful pain he told the maid where the potatoes were and said what was to be done with the frame if the sun came out.'* "

As One Countryman to Another

QUALMS

No one believes that fox-hunting will come to an end in England in a hurry. It is buttressed not only by an investment of more than £15,000,000 and a yearly expenditure of £8,750,000 – the figures of a well known sportsman – but by the support of a succession of rich newcomers to country life, to whom hunting offers many attractions. Riding to hounds is glorious exercise and calls for pluck, fine horsemanship and good fellowship. It gives great pleasure to a large number of people and it is cherished as a survival of 'good old days' which never were except on Christmas cards ... All the virtues do not reside in the bosoms of critics of hunting.

Yet no close student of rural conditions can doubt that the feeling against fox-hunting is growing in many parts of the country ... A large proportion of the public has increasing qualms over the cruelty with which hunting so often culminates. It is no use pretending that cruelty does not frequently occur. With regard to the fox, it is established beyond all question by Press reports, news in the sporting papers, and admissions in sporting books and in hunting men's magazine articles ...

Although many good men and women who hunt do not feel themselves culpable in respect of the cruelties that are unhappily frequent in organized sport, and it is easy for men and women who have no inclinations towards sport to be censorious of sportsmen, we could not without hypocrisy conduct a review of rural progress if we hesitated to express our conviction that, at this time of day, such cruelties are a reproach to civilization, ill accord with the kindliness and good feeling of the English countryside, and are a stumbling block in the way of school teachers, who endeavour to teach the young, and the county authorities, who endeavour to enforce among adults, humane treatment of birds and animals ... We believe that drag-hunting ought to be steadily substituted for fox-hunting and beagling ...

AND THE CURE

In an early number of *The Countryman* 'R.H.R.' suggested that the qualities which hunting develops in young men, in their own and the national interest, could be equally cultivated by aeroplaning ... The townsman who leaves hunting for airmanship may lose the considerable benefit of gaining an acquaintance with rural conditions, and the countryman may miss the pleasure of association with horses and hounds; but in zest and adventure, in demands on resolution and skill, in the joy of speed and of unfolding landscape, in healthful glow, in the opportunity of trying his powers against his fellows, in general variety of experience and in national advantage, the air has everything to offer over the chase. And the satisfactions obtained are not alloyed by something which, nowadays, it must be admitted, is just a little barbaric, just a little selfish, just a little anachronistic … The hunting man and woman, as represented in their literature, are human, mettlesome and courageous, but they are not always particularly brainy. The young countrymen and countrywomen who are taking to the air have mentally as well as physically a wider outlook … In a few years it will seem strange that more people did not realize that its [the small aeroplane's] advent in the countryside was as certain as the coming of the motor, the telephone and electric light and power, and that when it arrives it must draw from hunting some of the most gallant and enterprising spirits of both sexes. Can hunting long survive, in some districts at any rate, the air attack, the economic attack and the humane attack?

Fox-hunting was a source of contention right from the earliest days of The Countryman. *Here, a series of letters (largely against) in January 1936 included this little dig at the sport by the Society for the Prevention of Cruel Sports.*

A Foxhunter plants a covert

buys some fox cubs

releases them

and tell us he hunts to keep foxes down

The Country House Aeroplane

COUNTRYWOMEN WHO FLY
BY THE HON. LADY BAILEY, D.B.E.

It is rather wonderful to think that, if you get a really grilling day in the summer, you can pull out your small aeroplane, start it up, take off and fly yourself down to the seaside for the day or for a morning or merely for a bathe. Given a suitable field, with clear approaches and a small shed in which to house a light aeroplane, and there is the possibly [*sic*] of flying to any town in England or Europe or North Africa which possesses an aerodrome. And, of course, still further afield if you make sure that the petrol and oil for your light aeroplane are to be had. If you want merely to go up to Scotland, you need about three and a half hours from London to get to Edinburgh. On a fine day some of the scenery up north, when seen from up above, is very beautiful. You can fly over the wild lake country in Cumberland and look down on the islands between the Scottish and Irish coasts …

No one, I feel, can fully realise what the possession of an aeroplane means until he or she has tried it. I hope many women will try it, because the joys are so many and the interests and opportunities so world-wide and immense …

Also I think that if people use flying and the private ownership of aeroplanes reasonably, they can advance aviation in Britain enormously and help to show what air travel will mean on the great Empire air routes.

A FARMER WHO BOUGHT A £1,350 CAR

[*A man who farmed in East Anglia did remarkably well, retiring in the fourth year of World War I with a considerable sum, well into five figures. He retired in 1918 at the age of 63 'to travel', and was 75 when he wrote the full story of how to succeed at farming, starting from nothing. His long article included the following invaluable advice:*]
I would not advise any farmer to take more land than he can canter round before breakfast (as I used to) and attend to carefully. If prosperous he had better invest surplus in Consols, etc., and forget it!

1931

An Angler's Conscience

BY 'SALFARIO'

When I was very young I read that Nimrod was a mighty hunter. I was interested. Afterwards I was allowed to read Fennimore Cooper. I was thrilled. Then they told me that the surest, quickest way to catch rabbits was to put salt on their tails. I crawled stealthily through the woods; I was a reincarnation of Nimrod and Yellow Hawk. But I caught no rabbits. I was told that the trout I saw in our village stream could be caught. It was suggested that a piece of string, a bent pin, a worm were all that was required. I caught no trout that way. There were sisters who laughed. Their laughter did not hurt much. It merely spurred my will to be a hunter!

I determined that the day would come when I should snare and outwit and catch these things. And the day did come. I would have you know that there was nothing unkind in this will to snare, outwit and catch. The will, the thought, the concentrated effort needed to do these things did me no harm as a boy. Would you learn restraint? To wait, to watch?

That there is a time, a second even, when you should control, hold in, hold back? And another moment when your action, your decision must be as quick, as startling as the flash of a salmon's tail? That there is great value in being quiet and unseen? That there is reward to him who waits and watches and is patiently persistent? Then learn to match all the sense you have against all that God has blessed a trout with. And in the combat you will learn these things, at least in part.

Perhaps the provision of these things to hunt, to try our skill on, to test our wits, is one of the subtle means prepared by Nature for our good, for all creatures' good. Maybe we should all be better if we had to hunt our food. No one believes that the domesticated animal is wholly an improvement on the wild one. I find no trace of the idea of killing in any of this development. I was never interested in killing – even flies. But there is only one end to hunting – one proper end, one noble end. I have suggested a nobler end than being killed to be eaten.

There is an aspect of this idea of killing which is curious. It is best illustrated by a story once told me by a butcher. A worthy and kindly man he was, of the type that only lives now in villages – small and remote villages. He employed a new boy, who, in the early stages of his training, was told to stick a lamb. The boy boggled at this horrid job. He said he couldn't. My friend the butcher did not upbraid or even chide him. He appeared to agree with the boy and told him to release the animal and let it out in the pasture near by. Later in the day he told the boy to go and catch that lamb. It was not until a long time had gone by that the boy returned, breathless and well nigh exhausted, dragging the lively creature behind him. Said he, 'I'll stick the little devil now if you like!' I would not suggest that this story of the butcher's boy explains why I have no compunction about the killing of a trout or salmon. But I do admit it indicates my attitude of mind.

I have more than once said that it is only the fool trout that gets caught – and the fool salmon for that matter. Everything is in their favour, and, brainless as they are, there are a hundred reasons why they should never be caught. In almost every case a capture is directly attributable either to their greed or carelessness. You will see that I almost argue that Nature made these things for the catching – I cannot think for what else they could have been made so devoid of feeling as humans know it. I do not argue that they are food for men – though indeed they are. None of these obvious reasons satisfy my attitude. I am satisfied, knowing as I do that a fish, fairly caught, fairly deserves its fate …

MOTORING one night recently I saw, on rounding a bend, that the whole roadway ahead was dotted with pairs of tiny green points, gleaming iridescently in the darkness, and continually appearing and disappearing. I found that I had met an army of rats on the move, and that the green points were the creatures' eyes. The gleaming brilliance of animals' eyes, when caught in the glare of headlights, is a common sight to motorists. A cat's, a dog's or a rabbit's eyes usually shine green. The eyes of a fox flash back bright crimson, the eyes of a bullock a kind of rich amber.

The Country House Aeroplane

THE AUTOGIRO

To many of us the most interesting thing in aeroplaning just now is the Autogiro or 'windmill' aeroplane, as it is popularly called. The trouble about aeroplanes with most people is not what they may do in the air but the rate at which they may hit the ground. The Autogiro cannot descend rapidly and it is, therefore, impossible to hit the ground on descending. The Autogiro may be conceived as an aeroplane with a parachute attached. The four blades which rotate with the forward speed of the machine, or with its downward descent, have a lifting effect which enables the machine not only to fly at very low speeds but virtually to stop and descend vertically. The Autogiro development is of particular interest to country residents, for it makes it possible for an aeroplane to land in quite a small area. A three-acre field would probably be quite sufficient. With skill it would even be possible to land on a tennis court, though this would be trick flying and would be impracticable for the private owner. More room, however, is required by the Autogiro for rising from the ground. In taking off, about thirty yards run is required. This will probably be considerably improved upon when the rotary blades are made to rotate mechanically. At present they are moved by the wind-stream set up by the propeller.

One of the virtues of the Autogiro is its extreme simplicity of handling. Although the ordinary normal flying training should be undertaken by any prospective owner, an Autogiro owner has the comforting knowledge that, however unskilful he may be, it is almost impossible for him to crash on landing. Unless he should fly directly into an obstacle, such as a house or a tree, he should always be able to get the machine down to the ground without serious damage. Even with a parachute, it is possible, if one lands awkwardly, to break a leg, but the Autogiro descends at less than the speed of a man landing by parachute. There is, therefore, a large margin for safety, and only considerable clumsiness, extending almost to stupidity, would produce any personal damage to the pilot.

The Autogiro, it should be understood, is not the same in principle as a Helicopter. The Helicopter might be described as a machine with propellers which lift it mechanically from the ground. The Autogiro obtains its lift by a combined forward and upward movement, the lift being obtained from the angle of the rotary blades as the machine travels through the air.

The inventor, Cierva, is a Spaniard. Although most of the experiments have been carried out in this country, the machine is making progress in America ...

The Trend of Agricultural Thinking

THE HORSES' POINT OF VIEW

My corn was tangled, and what is worse, grown in. Thank goodness
I have a tractor. Cutting tangled corn with horses is a terrible business.
People who talk about its being so sad that horses are being given up,
they are so fond of horses, they are not interested in farming without
horses, etc., simply don't know what they are talking about. If I were
a horse there is certain work like ploughing which I should enjoy.
When one is young and fit continuous steady work, like rowing or
cutting through trees with a crosscut saw, gives a sort of quiet joy which
ploughing must give to a good pair of horses. They probably chat to each
other occasionally in some way or other as they go along; but cutting
tangled corn on a hot day with torturing flies and the constant hacking
and backing to get the binder out of tangles must be a torturing job.
Any horse lover with imagination must hate to see it. Mechanization
makes the farming world fit for horses to live in by giving a few of them
pleasant healthy work and a decent life.

Farm-Owner

*The stark detail of the immemorial Cerne Giant, cut in the face
of the hill at Cerne Abbas, lately offended some male visitors,
who proceeded to Grundify it with grass sods. After they had gone
it was two women who removed the sods.*

1934

The Passing of the Years

1815. 'They tell me, miller, you're going to have one of those newfangled windmills.' 'Aye, parson,' said Sam Eldridge; 'it's no good going on wi' me old contraption. I can't manage all the grist they brings me. A windmill it's got to be, and there bain't no place to put 'im except up on the Down where there's some wind. I'm sorry, sir, if it's going to jigger up your view of the Downs, but ...'

1932. 'Yes,' said Charlie Eldridge, the miller, Sam's grandson, 'I were for scrapping the old mill, it's no use to me; but here's this Society come along, and they say 'twould be a sin to do away with a fine old landmark. It don't seem like sense, but they're going to put 'im in order, and they're going to pay me – well, they're doing the thing 'andsome.' 'What's all this about these 'ere pylons, Bill?' asked the blacksmith. 'Why, Tom, they wants to give us 'lectric light, and it means

they've got to put up big tower things to carry the wires, and some of these London folks say it's goin' to spoil the Downs ...'

2034. In the inn the television set was presenting an impassioned appeal by the President of the Society for the Protection of the Countryside. 'And now I come to the latest proposal made in the name of progress by our modern vandals, who wish to take down the line of graceful early twentieth-century pylons on the Downs. My Society is going to fight this sacrilege with all its power. Although the structures do not serve any practical purpose in these days of radio distribution of power, these fine old creeper-grown monuments of the past stand against the sky as one of a fast diminishing number of relics of an England that is gone, and we propose to buy the ground each pylon stands upon.' *A.L.J.H.*

1935

Why I Live in the Country

BY ST. JOHN ERVINE

I live in the country because I like living in the country. The thrill of being one of eight million pasty-faced persons who are crowded into the smallest space that will hold eight million pasty-faced persons is one that I have never been able to experience. If I were a dictator I should go about with a knacker's hammer and knock down two-thirds of the houses in London and I should not greatly break my heart if the inhabitants of them were buried in the ruins. I should do still better, I think, if I were to knock down three-thirds of them. I lived in London for the better part of twenty-seven years, and I can claim, therefore, to have some knowledge of life in that wen. There are a few parts of it where I would be willing, if heavily bribed, to live again, but the largest part of London is an offence to the eye and sometimes an offence to the nose. I hate the sight of all those smug streets, stretching dully into the distance, as I hate the agitated way in which everybody moves about. There they go, hurrying like hell nowhere! And rending the air with their din as they hurry. The legend that one is at the centre of things in London is one of those astonishing legends which delude the silly and amuse the intelligent. How many of the eight million persons in London are at the centre of things? Not enough, I believe, to populate a large village. And what, pray, is the centre of things? … London is a boring place, I see more bored men and women in its streets in one day than I see in my neighbourhood in one year … London is a headachy place, stuffy and noisy … Nerve-wracked townsmen, overwrought by the sound of their resonant streets, come into the country and have the audacity to say that they cannot bear its noise, although their ear-drums have almost been split and their nerves torn to shreds by city sounds. Country noises are good noises, natural noises, evenly distributed and made comfortable to the ear by the space in which they can vibrate.

[Editor's note: This piece continues with a rant against litter dropped by hikers and motorists, and against the roadhouses and B&Bs to accommodate them. V.L.P.]

The Trend of Agricultural Thinking

STERILIZATION OF MILK BY SOUND

The devastating effect of the noises of the trumpet was demonstrated long ago. It is possible to evoke sounds of extraordinary shrillness and intensity. Leslie A. Chambers and Newton Gaines have succeeded in extracting sounds which are deadly from a nickel tube placed in a strong electromagnetic field in resonance with a 2,000-volt oscillating power circuit. Water fleas are destroyed in a second. These noises turn the blood, as the French say. Red blood cells persecuted by them for ten minutes go to pieces altogether and white blood cells endure no better. Nor do bacteria. It is with such noises that Chambers and Gaines have done such good deeds. Milk, pullulating with micro-organisms, placed in a flask and held half under water close to the open end of the noisy nickel tube, becomes relatively pure in a very short time. In one case the milk contained twelve million organisms per cubic centimetre, say 6,000 million to the pint. After forty minutes 96 per cent of the micro-organisms were no more – the angel of death spread his wings on the flask! Of course, even so, the milk was still densely populated with micro-organisms – there survived about 240 million in a pint ... Dr. Chambers has been devoting the last two or three years to perfecting this method of milk sterilization. He has produced a 'sonizer' which can deal with 1,500 gallons of milk in an hour with a reduction of bacterial content of from 90 to 100 per cent ... To pasteurise milk is to rob it of virtue: not to pasteurise milk is to ignore a possible avenue and risk of infection of the body of the child. Sonization, if the word may pass, will preserve the virtue and destroy the microbe, thereby resolving the doctor's dilemma.

Frederick Keeble

1936

Farming Fifty Years Hence

BY SIR DANIEL HALL, F.R.S.

To accept an invitation to prophesy concerning the condition of agriculture fifty years on is to walk into an open trap. But at any rate I shall not be there to be pilloried …

I can recall some of the farming of fifty or even sixty years ago. At bottom it was not so very different … Details have been changed; the principles remain unaffected. During the last fifty years the one novelty which stands out in the English countryside has been the advent of the tractor.

If one may interpret the future by the past I feel pretty certain that fifty years hence farmers will be very much the same sort of people as they are to-day or as they were half a century ago. They will be individualists, firm in their own opinions, constituting a class somewhat apart. They will be conscious that their occupation possesses an element of reality, something that is self-satisfying and more worthy of a man than other businesses and professions, even if it leads to less money. They will share the sense of superiority which the country gentleman feels towards his neighbours who have newly acquired their estates. But I fear that, more than ever, farmers and farming will have dropped out of the minds of the vastly greater urban population; it will be interesting to read about in books and articles like the birds and the wild flowers about which we make so much ado to-day but otherwise outside the general stream of life.

Indeed if things go on as they have been moving during the last fifty years, over a great part of England there won't be much land left for farming. The cities are always spreading out, not merely for housing, but taking in the countryside for golf courses and lunatic asylums, for reservoirs and aerodromes. The demands of the Army and the Air Force are of no light order and are increasing as the newer arts of war require space in which to exercise. Between them they have defaced no inconsiderable portion of the countryside south of the Thames. We have still got to provide for the refuges into which London and the other towns will be evacuated when the bombing begins.

This indeed leads to the final consideration which may nullify all prophecies. What about war! The next war that seems so near and so threatening, the war that is going to be directed against the civil population, whoever nominally may win, will mean the end of Western European society as we now know it. Agriculture of a sort may again become the leading, almost the only industry; we may slip back into the society that medievalists postulated – the King (or the dictators) to rule, the soldiers to fight, and the labourers to till the fields! But these are nightmares engendered by reading the pronouncements of the dictators of the day. Let us assume that children who play with fire do not always succeed in burning the house down.

… As the last twenty years have abundantly demonstrated, our farming community possesses great powers of adaptation to new conditions; the seeds of progress are there but whether they will develop quickly or slowly depends upon the national weather.

BY Dr. H.J. Denham,
Director of the Institute for Research in Agricultural Engineering, Oxford

Sometimes I have a vision of a ragged man, a spear slung on his back, ploughing with a starvecrow horse. It might come to this, given a general war and the breakdown of our civilization. But assuming that we and the others learn sense I am forced to the conclusion that without an entirely new break, something as big as the introduction of a new source of power, progress will consist only of minor modifications, even if the outstanding economic problems are solved as well. Ironically enough, these new breaks seem to occur in our civilization only under the stimulus of a war. I am coming more and more to see farming practice as a continuous fight against the elements, with a growing and formidable list of scientific discoveries as our chief armament: and of late I have been wondering seriously whether the possibility of even the smallest control of some factors of the weather is as chimaeric as the meteorologists have always maintained. After all, the forces which have upset our weather this season originated in a spot or spots on the sun subtending a very minute angle as seen from the earth. If only the cause of the relationship of sunspot activity to rainfall could be established, we have immense resources of power – our generating stations standing idle most of the night – but this is sheer speculation. Given hostile planes spraying mustard gas over the country, it would be worth while being able to induce cloudbursts at will, and no project for doing so would be too insane to consider. Turning back to our problem, we have huge stores of knowledge which we cannot afford to use. Plenty no longer means prosperity. If we can solve this one paradox in the next fifty years, we can start thinking seriously about real progress.

(continued overleaf)

BY A.H. BROWN,
Hampshire farmer

To attempt to look at the future is more important than wasting time on the past. It is certain that before long the State will own all the agricultural land, and that of itself will change the whole psychology of the farmer ... I expect to see the coming generation of farmers better educated and more like city people. That may be good or bad, but I have never yet heard of anyone who admires a country cottage or a country accent admit a wish to live in the cottage as it is, or who would copy the accent or allow his children to do so. All homes will have electric light and power and running water. Wages will compare favourably with those of industry and commerce, and there will be adequate holidays and pensions. Although production will be doubled, the number of workers on the land will probably be fewer. There will be no smallholders and no producer-retailers; distribution will be a State service and conducted on rational lines ... I expect to see a great extension of marketing schemes, with increased co-operation between organized producers and consumers. I do not agree that soon the whole countryside south of London will be a playing field. The whole of the actual coast may be, but there will be very large areas untouched by the speculator. It is to be hoped that the picturesque insanitary cottages will be pulled down and modern ones built, with enough bedrooms. Population will decline, although a larger proportion will live in the country ... Every village will have its recreation room. I can't see the churches being used, except as objects of interest and often beauty. Every community will have its playing field laid out with borders of flowers and trees. The country people themselves will be of finer physique through better feeding and gymnastics. There will be a revival of singing, dancing and acting; less scandal because life will be fuller.

COUNTRYMAN CLUB

THE VERNACULAR AS WRITTEN – Is this bill, said to have been rendered by a westcountryman, new?

			s.	d.
Orsafada	...	...	1	6
Aforim	...	...		3
Agetenovenomagen	...	...		6
			2	3

Translation: Horse half a day, hay for him, a-getting of him home again.   A.P.

How to Deal with Rabbits

If Mr. Lockley wishes to exterminate his rabbits, the following method is inexpensive and certain. Select a dozen sites on rising ground and preferably in sandy soil. Dig a hole at each side 3 feet long, 2 feet wide and 1½ feet deep, taking care that the bottom of the hole is well above the level of the surface of the surrounding land on at least two sides. Cut two shallow trenches 8 or 9 feet long leading into the hole, in which lay 4 inch agricultural pipes. Line the inside of the hole with bricks, letting in a 4 inch pipe in two or three places in the wall. Put hay, straw, fern or heather in the central space to make a dry bed; hay is best as it is food as well as bed. Place a wooden lid over the top and cover with the sods originally over. Place a fairly heavy stone near the mouth of each inlet – which must always run uphill into the holes – with which to stop the entrances. Then make a mop with a shaft the length of your inlets. In a fortnight rabbits will begin lying up on your bracken or heather, but it is well to give them time to acquaint their friends and relations. Take your mop, stop one inlet with a stone, push your mop up the other and lift the lid of your trap. The rabbits inside will be out of sight either in the pipes let into the walls or down the inlet through which your mop has not been pushed. Let out any birds or extraneous beast; put your hand (with a glove on) up one of the short drain pipes; pull out a rabbit and, if it is a doe, kill it – not too near the hole. If a buck, let it go. Having investigated all your drain pipes, pull your mop from inlet no. 1, stop the inner end with a stone, replace the lid of your trap and push your mop up inlet no. 2. Proceed as before until your trap is empty, remove the stone and mop from the two inlets and proceed to your next trap. Thus, no other animal or bird is hurt on account of your rabbits, and does are caught and killed in the most humane way. Your released bucks would return to the trap, bringing friends. They would soon find a shortage of does and fight to the death over those that remained, and would seek out nests of young ones and kill these in order to bring the mothers on heat again. When all the does are dead – say in one year – the remaining old bucks would be caught in the traps or shot in the open. This plan has been tried with success.

A.J. Homer Hawkins

1937

Birds and Men on Heligoland

BY R.M. LOCKLEY

From Cuxhaven I crossed last October to Helgoland (the German spelling of the island's name) in a surprisingly grand steamer, in two and a half hours. On the way over an old Helgolander with whom I became acquainted on board prepared me for the surprise of finding an islet half as small as Skokholm supporting a population of 3,000. He was returning to his native island after a long exile in Britain. He had never lost British citizenship – that right had been guaranteed him when England exchanged Helgoland for Zanzibar. He was excited as the red cliffs loomed up – the coast of Germany is flat and dyke-bound – and began humming a little rhyme which he translated for me:

> Green is that Land
> Red is that Cliff,
> White is that sand:
> That is the flag of Helgoland.

The native dialect, a curious hybrid of English and Scandinavian, is now dying out under the influence of 'pure' Nazi German. The Helgolanders paid no taxes during the English

occupation, nor was any man obliged to serve in the British Army. But my acquaintance, with several friends, had joined the Queen's Navy. As a port, Helgoland was the second free harbour in Europe (Copenhagen is the first). The people were not interfered with in the least.

When the Helgoland-Zanzibar change-over took place a clause in the Anglo-German agreement exempted all men born under English rule from service in the German army or navy. The Germans instantly began fortifications on the grand scale. The tops of the cliffs were bricked or tiled over to prevent rain washing away the edges of the very soft rock, and a two-way lift and a tunnel brought the upper and lower town together.

On August 1st, 1914, a large steamer anchored off the island. It had come to evacuate the 2,000 inhabitants. They were given an hour to pack what could be carried in the hand. Everything else must be left until the war was won in a few weeks' time. All men who had formerly served in the British services were summarily arrested, a precaution illustrating German thoroughness, for Britain had not yet declared war upon Germany! Although these men could not be required to join the German services, they knew too much of the coast and the fortifications to be permitted the opportunity to escape abroad.

Helgoland had, by tradition, seven havens or anchorages, and numerous streams and settlements in the year 800 AD. In 1649 actual survey reduced the traditional extent about a quarter. Since then the sea has steadily encroached, and at the present day the soft cliffs are still tumbling into the water, despite breakwaters and extensive underpinning at great cost.

On December 5th, 1918, a dismal winter day, a steamer left Hamburg with the sadly reduced 1914 population of Helgoland. Those who had the heart to claim compensation for lost business and damaged property were reminded that, even if they were paid a billion marks, they could scarcely buy a loaf of bread with it, so low had the mark fallen. Then work came unexpectedly to the penniless islanders. Under the supervision of English officers the fortifications and the submarine base were to be destroyed completely. It took three years to destroy the moles, plug the tunnels, and sabotage the machinery. The English officers are well remembered in Helgoland, not so much for their friendliness that made them so popular, but for the extraordinary circumstance that when off duty they joined in the life and amusements and wore the clothes of the civilian people!

Twelve years after the destruction of the fortifications the Germans are rebuilding them on an even more gigantic scale. The dynamiting during the demolition was bad enough, but when the great new guns speak the crumbling cliffs may give way. Still, rebuilding means work, and probably there are over 3,000 people crowded to-day upon less than the 50 acres of the residential quarter. About 400 children attend the morning school. There is no afternoon school. When pleasure cruisers call in summer, 9,000 people may throng the narrow streets.

It was Helgoland as a bird observatory that I had come to see …

EPISTLES FROM AN OLD HOMESTEAD
BY HUMPHREY JOHN

… I found myself lunching in a lovely manor in the south country a fortnight ago: four motor cars and a butler – that size. My hostess had started her day at five, in the dairy, and had been at work ever since, ending with the cooking of the food we were eating: she herself did the dairy, the poultry, the laundry (all at home), the cooking and most of the housework, and all because she liked doing it. I wish there were more nowadays like her: we are all getting so much too much into the habit of being dependent on everybody else.

The Diary of a Fruit Farmer

MAR. 14, 1937

A friend tells me that the LNER, having for years noticed that the growth of weeds on the permanent way between Holyhead and London was always stronger on the down line than on the up, eventually traced their vigour to the drip from the loaded fish vans. Which reminds me of the story of the lady who said fish manure had done wonders in her garden, but she couldn't for the life of her think how it was collected.

APR. 8, 1937

Saw a Grecian cystus which carries gum upon its leaves. The Greeks drive their Angora goats through the bushes and at leisure comb out the gum from the goats' hair. The gum keeps dental plates in position — sometimes.

APR. 23, 1937

Heard about a new virus to destroy rabbits, called myxomotosis cuniculae. It is being tried since October on an island in the Atlantic, but up to date the sea has been too rough to allow the inventor to land. He hopes to find all the rabbits dead. If successful the bowler hat may become extinct or the sign manual of the plutocrat.

JULY 26, 1937

Tried to get our local dentist to take a tooth out for me, but he is a great cricketer and regrets that he will be too busy as cricket week starts to-day. To draw stumps on the opening day would of course be out of the question.

Natural History at Downing Street

BY THE PRIME MINISTER [NEVILLE CHAMBERLAIN]

Naturally *The Countryman* is interested first and foremost in the country, but there is a *rus in urbe* where I write, in which sometimes reminders of the country may be visible for those who have eyes to see.

The old garden between Downing Street and the Horse Guards Parade has existed for at least two hundred and fifty years, and perhaps it retains for that reason some traces of more rural surroundings. Only a few days ago, I was delighted to find resting on the trunk of a small hawthorn tree, a specimen of the beautiful, but rarely seen, Leopard Moth, its long, white, blue-black spotted wings folded over its back. The larva of this insect is a wood-borer, and, as far as I know, there is no tree in the garden which would be suitable for its food. Nevertheless, from its perfect condition, I am sure it could not have made any long flight, and it must have passed its earlier stages somewhere in the neighbourhood.

When I first came here in January of 1936, I at once affixed a nesting-box to one of the trees in the garden. Nothing happened for a long time, but last March I saw a pair of blue, or perhaps I should say, black tits, for they were a grimy couple, flitting about the branches of a lime tree. Shortly afterwards they were flying in and out of the box. I did not have time to make any examination till the weekend after I had become Prime Minister, when on looking into the box, I found the nest completed and three eggs in it. Unfortunately, I saw little more movement, and looking again in June, found that the nest was deserted and the three eggs had been reduced to two. Now what is the solution of the mystery of the vanished egg?

Did the tits themselves carry it away, or did some marauder make off with it? I remember, long years ago, my mother's twin sister, a lady much beloved by me for her sweet disposition and her keen humour, related a conversation with her venerable gardener. Said my aunt, 'John, I see the blackbirds have been busy again with the cherries,' 'May be, Ma'am,' the old man replied, and then with an indescribably sly chuckle, he added, 'but I fancy some two legged blackbirds must have been round here.' I wonder if some animal of the same species went off with my tits' egg.

1938-1946

The Challenges of War

A second world war had long been threatened. In the late 1930s some three-quarters of agricultural income was derived from livestock and a quarter from arable farming. The war would change that balance dramatically, and even the threat of war was an impetus to plough up grassland in favour of growing cereals. In 1938 the average weekly earnings of an agricultural worker amounted to about 35 shillings (£1.75): labourers were leaving the farms for better prospects elsewhere in large numbers. In 1939 there were only 150 combine harvesters in the country and just a few progressive dairy farms were milking their cows by machine rather than by hand. There were more than 15,000 tractors at work but the horse was still widely used as a source of farming power; there were 11 horses to every tractor. Many farms and rural villages had no mains electricity or mains water – a situation that would continue in a surprisingly large number of places until well after the end of the war, even in villages not far from the big cities and towns.

The summer of 1939 was one of the warmest on record. War was declared on 3 September, and it would be fought in the countryside by farmers and their workers as well as by the armed forces. The race was on to produce food for a nation whose imports were dramatically curtailed, and the government and its agents encouraged, or even forced under threat of loss of their land, all farmers to aim for maximum production at all costs. The landscape was changing fast, and there was also a big influx of strangers into the countryside – armies in camps or on the march to the coast, new aerodromes for fighter planes, land girls and conscientious objectors to help with the farming side by side with prisoners of war, and of course evacuees from the cities billeted with local villagers and farmers. The Great War had already shaken up the social structure of rural areas; this second war would have an even greater effect and would further blur the demarcation between rural and urban living. And that process was reflected in the pages of *The Countryman*.

Before the war, *The Countryman* continued to advise those who wanted to make their own little patches of land productive. It introduced a new slot for 'The Home Acre – Making the Most of a Bit of Land', a popular subject for which was bee-keeping. It continued, for the time being, various series from individual farmers and introduced the splendid Clyde Higgs, whose regular and long-running column of 'Farmer's Ruminations' looked at farming on a large scale: he himself ran ten farms and a well known dairy with great commercial success. The journal also received occasional pieces from esteemed men such as C.S. Orwin and Sir Daniel Hall. Other well known occasional contributors include H.G. Wells and H.E. Bates, and a whole host of famous names contributed to a series 'Who prop in these bad days my mind', in which they wrote about what they read and what they did to distract themselves from the horrors of this new war.

Animals and birds had always been popular subjects among the readers, who were now invited to contribute their observations to a new section, 'Wild Life and Tame', which covered everything from wildlife to the behaviour of cats and dogs and farm animals. The natural history element was also covered in articles about tame foxes, the effect of fog on flying birds and, more dramatically, the avian death toll caused by the beams from lighthouses and searchlights.

At the beginning of the war, the editor had decided that the conflict should not be mentioned in the pages of *The Countryman*. This attempt at cocooning the readers from harsh reality did not last for more than an issue or two, and a good picture of what it was like to live in Britain during the war can be built up from hundreds of personal observations ranging from the trite to the more serious, albeit usually told with that typical British sense of humour. But in a way the editor had been right: the countryside would continue its way of life despite the war; the birds would still nest and sing; the livestock would still munch and be ornery; the fields would still be cultivated; the seasons would still turn as they had always done, and no bombs would stop them. It was a way of life that the armed forces were serving to protect, and therefore it continued to be celebrated in all its quirky ways.

J.W.R.S. had spent years carefully building up a goodly number of selected advertisers to keep his publication afloat, and it is intriguing to see how they coped during the war. Many of them had to maintain a profile for their customers even though they might have nothing to sell them. For example, Cadburys had to explain that sugar rationing had reduced the amount it could include in its products, and that anyway the 'sustaining powers' of its chocolate were needed for the troops (four-fifths of the company's total output went to 'Government priorities'). The Allied Forces were also a priority for Viyella's garments and this company could only remind people of their famous name and promise to return to production once the war was over – which they did with humour. It was certainly a test of the copy-writers' ingenuity.

Surprisingly, the war gave a huge boost to the popularity of *The Countryman*. Many people helped to ensure that it was circulated to troops serving overseas and in the fleet, to remind them of home and of just what it was they were fighting to protect, and those left at home grew even more appreciative of their beloved countryside. This popularity continued to grow after the war and the print-run would reach 80,000 copies per issue in 1955 – still at the original price of half-a-crown. During the war, with acute shortages in everything, including paper, the number of pages was reduced considerably (down to 152 in the spring of 1944, for example) but by using a smaller type face and a denser layout on the page, there was very little loss in the actual content of the journal. It was more than ready to meet the fresh challenges of the next decade of its life.

1938

My Island and Our Life There

BY R.M. LOCKLEY

The first Lockley contributions – they have been appearing quarter by quarter since 1931 – bore this heading. For the present issue the 'In Search of an Island' series is interrupted in order that we may learn more of the bird and animal – as well as the human – life of the island of Skokholm, in describing which the author first made his reputation as an ornithologist and naturalist.

... *April 18.* In the evening four rabbits were driven into a long-net, inoculated with the virus producing myxomatosis, and released. This disease is entirely fatal and specific. In controlled field experiments by Sir Charles Martin, who has made a study of its virulence, it has completely wiped out thickly populated artificial warrens of wild rabbits. But twice now – autumn 1936, and summer 1937 it has failed in the natural, less crowded warrens on Skokholm. It appears to be too fatal, killing those inoculated and those in the same burrows with them before they have had a chance to spread the contagion to inmates of other burrows ... If I could only exterminate the rabbits – and this had seemed at first a quick and ideal way – I should take heart to improve the land and run a sheep farm on the island. But at present the wretched rabbits poison the land, devouring the best grasses and wild clovers, and leaving nothing but moss, thistles and ragwort.

> " *The townsman, watching the tractor ploughing up the wheat stubble, asked what was being done, and when told, said, 'Do you not want the wheat to come up again next year?'* "

FROM DAY TO DAY

* Am told that an American farm tractor sold in this country has been tested up to 67 m.p.h.!
* My memory of Ramsay MacDonald is of his coming, with outstretched hand, through the doorway of a book-lined parlour (of Joseph Duncan, secretary of the Scottish Farm Servants' Union). A tall, handsome Highland chief of a man, fresh from a second-hand bookshop, who sat down on a stool by the fire, and poured out, as he smoked, cordial but pawky appreciation of a friend.

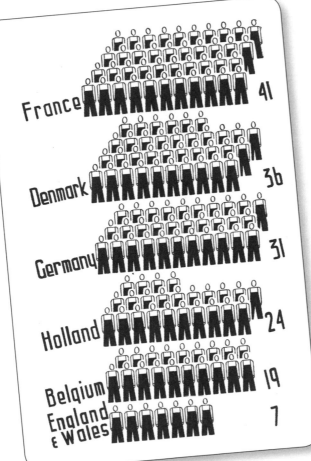

A diagram by Barlow in 1938 illustrating the percentage of the population on the land in various European regions, with England & Wales way down the list.

The Diary of a Fruit Farmer

Sept. 5, 1937

I read that German scientists have valued the titmouse at £7 a nest. Each hatch of young birds is estimated to eat 4,800 caterpillars, thus saving 4,800 apples (valued at 2d. per pound) at £7. I think we should go back further. If a bee pollenizes ten flowers a minute in a ten-hour season of suitable weather a hive of only 5,000 free working bees might visit and set 30,000,000 flowers — over 6,000 times as many apples for caterpillars to bite or titmouse to save. Should we therefore value a hive of bees at over £40,000? Figures are very deceptive. Caterpillars are only one enemy and all apples are not worth 2d. a pound.

Dec. 26, 1937

Meet Mrs. 'Price, who is my daughter-in-law's daily help down in Worcestershire. She gets up at 4 a.m., cleans her cottage, puts up husband's midday meal (he is a cowman), cooks breakfast for 5.30 a.m., clears it, cooks and lays supper ready for her husband to warm up. Leaves home by 6 and cycles two and a half miles to collect the daily papers, which she delivers locally in addition to helping the postman with mails. At 9 she starts day work, does all the cleaning, cooking and laundrywork, asking only a slice of bread and butter and a cup of tea, and leaves for home at 8.30 p.m. Bed at 11 and works every Sunday morning in her garden.

> *When auntie asked what the Anti-Litter League was the bright young niece replied, 'Oh, don't you know, auntie dear – birth control for dogs, of course!'*

In Search of an Island – North Ronaldshay

BY R.M. LOCKLEY

VICTIMS OF THE FLASHING LIGHT

One evening we borrowed bicycles and pedalled to the lighthouse. All day there had been a south-east wind and heavy cloud, and now it was beginning to drizzle. Such conditions, succeeding a spell of fine weather, throw the migrating bird out of its airy path. As we rode towards the tall tower, birds were already flashing like stars in those 16 rays which revolve around North Ronaldshay light. We carried sacks to hold any birds we might capture as they fell dazzled from the glass.

The drizzle thickened. Lights in the distant cottages became dim, then vanished. We hoped it would not grow so misty as to necessitate the use of the fog signal. Its ear-splitting blast, added to the cruel darkness on such nights, must inflict the final misery upon the tortured migrating bird. It is little realized how terrible is this death-trap of the lighthouse. The slaughter which we witnessed on this night was, after all, but one of many such devastations at lighthouses up and down the coast each spring and autumn …

That night for five hours the tower of North Ronaldshay lighthouse resounded to the thuds of birds hurling themselves at the light, some directly upon the glazing and some upon the railings and stonework. Others seemed to make a last effort to leap clear, and these all too often crashed against the dome above or against the gallery rail. A thump, a flutter of feathers on the breeze, then a body dropping to leeward to hit pavement or earth with a second pitiful thud. They came in twos and threes, dozens and scores, rushing and wheeling through the 16 rays. Many, in trying to pass on the windward side, were wind-drifted instead with terrible force against the glass. Some birds arrived more gently, fluttering up to the light, and then, dazzled, dropping slowly downwards. These we picked up as they reached the ground, and put them into our sacks. We used a net and a lamp, and soon had 200 apparently sound and lively birds. Redwings … fieldfares … blackbirds and starlings … golden plover … the rain of killed, dying, or stunned birds continued … when, weary of watching the slaughter, we went home for an hour of sleep. We were back soon after sunrise. One quarter of the birds in the sacks were dead or dying of their wounds. We ringed and released the remainder … We tried to estimate the number of dead birds lying within a hundred yards to leeward of the lighthouse. They were certainly well over one thousand, not counting the many which must have been lying on the roofs of the buildings. Wading birds such as snipe and sandpiper had their long bills crumpled and shredded. The broken-winged and swollen-headed hopped about or crouched, most pitiful to see …

The Diary of a Fruit Farmer

July 18, 1938

A hint for those who propose to move trees which are on the large side. Always mark the north side of the tree and plant again with the mark in the same position. Orientation may be more important than people think.

Nov. 8, 1938

Pears have kept shockingly badly this season, and growers without gas storage have had to clear their fruit in a hurry. Talking of gas storage, America is said to have found that immersion of a dead-drunk for two hours in an atmosphere containing ten per cent of carbon dioxide gas is a complete cure. Apple-growers who have entered storage chambers at eight per cent concentration rather fancy that the drunk would be actually dead at the end of two hours.

Nov. 24, 1938

In a vast factory [in the Midlands] I watched the mixing of large and polished red, green, yellow and blue pills. Containing an almost fatal dose of croton oil, they will delight the artistic eye of the West African native, who will gladly pay the store-keeper a full day's pay for benefits conferred by a single specimen, in his lucky colour. The stomach and the bowel are the greatest dividend-payers of all time. Here I saw that (friend of my childhood the bitter aloe resin in bulk. The Somaliland native packs it in gourds, sometimes with a stone in the middle to add weight. It used to come sewn up in goat and monkey skins when furs were cheaper.

Nov. 25, 1938

In one of our cities am told that a round hen-egg is looked upon with suspicion. A consignment of Egyptian eggs contained many such, and within one was a baby crocodile.

The Home Acre – A Pool for Ideas

WHY WE NEED A HOME ACRE

Once I lived in a town. The milkman brought to my door rich milk, Cornish cream, new-laid eggs, pats of country butter, and appetizing cream cheeses. The butcher down the road sold prime English beef, home-raised lamb and veal, and in their season, plump roasting chickens and succulent ducklings, all cleaned, trussed and ready for the oven. Round the corner was a pork-butcher's where the pies, sausages, home-cured bacon and fine hams drew one irresistibly. Next door the greengrocer supplied early lettuces, vegetables fresh and crisp, apples – even English apples! – and potatoes graded and free from soil. I was a woman then who did not appreciate the amenities of town life. Now I live in the country whence, presumably, all these blessings flow. A farm fifty yards from my cottage cannot supply me with milk as the farmer is not a registered retailer. For cream, I must send to the nearest town, eight miles away. 'Eggs?' 'Grocer takes 'em all, ma'am.' Twice weekly a butcher brings from the nearest town an unappetizing assortment of chilled and frozen meat, which he and his youthful assistant fling about the van, as this customer and that disdain the sorry-looking joints. By the time he reaches me, the gory mess on the floor of the van would turn the heartiest meat-eater into a vegetarian … 'Could I have a boiling fowl?' I timidly ask the milk roundsman. 'Yes, I dare say you could,' he answers; then quickly adds, 'We don't pluck and dress them, have to do that yourself, ma'am.' Potatoes are difficult to obtain locally … Half a mile away there is a market garden, but all the produce from it is sent to town … In spring the village is gay with apple-blossom, but they are all cider apple trees   *M.T.*

COUNTRYMAN CLUB

THE PIG THAT FOLLOWED THE PLOUGH

While motoring through the country near Great Rollright, we saw what seemed to be a small pig following a plough, keeping his pace about six feet behind the ploughman. We stopped the car while the procession, two horses, plough, man and pig finished one row, turned and came back to where we waited. 'Yes, he likes a bit of company,' said the ploughman. *H.W.*

EPISTLES FROM AN OLD HOMESTEAD

BY HUMPHREY JOHN

There has been another upheaval of local feeling, this time about the new aerodrome, which a nearby municipality has planted on the best stretch of arable on the outskirts of the village, and which was taken over by the Air Ministry before it was completed. Nobody minds much about the arable, which of course was the subject of proper compensation, but it so happens that a little-used field path runs across the middle of it, a right of way going back into the mists of antiquity: and if there is one thing in the world over which we get worked up it is any sort of interference with a right of way. The aerodrome has set up ferocious warning notices, and the fire tender is kept busy warning what, to our annoyance, they insist on calling trespassers off the forbidden sward. There has been talk of putting up red flags, though whether to warn pilots that there are pedestrians about, or to warn pedestrians that there is flying in progress, is not quite clear …

The root of the whole matter seems to be that the footpaths have changed their function since the introduction of the bicycle. In distance, all these field paths are still the shortest route between the two points they connect, but in minutes they are now the longest because of their stiles. They are no longer used by men and women going to their daily tasks, but solely for the walking of leisure hours, for summer evenings and Sunday afternoons, and the long stages of courting, which even the bus and the pictures have not accelerated. It seems there is a standing rule that if a path is diverted it must not be lengthened: my own view is that under the new conditions the longer a path is the more it will be appreciated by its potential users, and the more stiles the merrier.

Simon Evans, the 'Postman Author' and occasional radio broadcaster, wrote about his life in the October 1938 issue, where the editor described being 'impressed by the strength of his personality and by his gallant and kindly fronting of life'. Badly wounded in the Great War, he became a postman and, despite his smashed legs and gassed lungs, he loved walking in the country and found refuge in this little hut, supplied by the Post Office to shelter its postmen on their long rounds. The hut was in Shropshire's Rea valley with a view of Titterstone Clee.

1939

Why Not a National Park in the Highlands?

BY THE EARL OF ONSLOW

I urge that an area in the Highlands should be made into a National Park because I believe that this is the most suitable spot. I need not say that I have no intention of proposing a rival to Dovedale or to any other part of the country which for its beauty, or for any other reason, might be usefully devoted to such a purpose.

We have a very interesting native fauna which if it is not protected must in time gradually disappear. A National Parks committee of the Council for the Preservation of Rural England and Wales, under the chairmanship of Mr. Norman Birkett, is established and a group is being formed of members of both Houses of Parliament. This Committee believes that the Government should: (1) declare that the establishment of National Parks is an essential national service, (2) set up, as chief and central agents, two National Parks Commissions (one for England and Wales and one for Scotland, with a joint committee co-ordinating the two), and (3) provide funds.

... I do not myself think that there is any place in England or Wales which would prove suitable for a National Park such as I propose ... A considerable acreage is absolutely essential ... and a nearby resident population would be a drawback to the preservation of many animals in a really wild state. Therefore the west coast of Scotland seems to be ideal ... The ideal spot would be an island such as I remember many years ago in the Gulf of Hauraki in New Zealand, acquired and stocked by Sir George Grey. But an island would not be a convenient place for the public to visit.

... Probably the most attractive animals in a Park will be the deer ... Other beasts which I think might well be added ... are the so-called park cattle. These, as is well known, exist in a wild state in their purest form at Chillingham ... Then in Scotland there are a few wild goats ... Foxes, badgers, stoats and weasels are common enough ... There would be no difficulty about them nor would there be about otters, provided of course the Park had streams, rivers and burns containing fish. But there are three species which are becoming very scarce and deserve every effort being made to retain them – the wild cat, the pine marten and the pole cat. … Seals are common enough on the west coast of Scotland, and if a bit of the Park were washed by the sea, it is possible that they might breed.

Is it desirable in a National Park to attempt to acclimatize animals which have become extinct in this country? … The elk, still found on the Continent, died out here in prehistoric times. But reindeer, wild pig and beaver have become extinct in England only within the last few centuries, and there seems no reason at all why they should not be re-introduced … Beavers were common in England until a few hundred years ago …

[Editor's note: In a later article there is also mention of reintroducing the wolf, a subject that would crop up again several decades later. Letters in favour of Onslow's idea for a Highlands National Park were printed in subsequent issues, albeit with various views on the types of fauna. Letters of criticism were mainly concerned with 'vermin' becoming a nuisance to neighbours, and conflicts between wildlife and tourists. V.I.P.]

FROM DAY TO DAY

* About 'rooinek' (red-neck), the name which the Boers who took Majuba called our young soldiers. A friend of mine who knew General Joubert, who was present at the fight, told me that the nickname was due to the way their necks caught the sun. Then Major Cecil Banbury kindly wrote to me that 'rooinek' was from the red collars of the troops' uniforms. To settle the matter I thought I would consult Sir Ian Hamilton, whose memorable experience on Majuba Hill he lately recounted on the wireless. He says: '"Rooinek" in my day was a term applied to any young Englishman whose fair skin used to be burnt scarlet. Our soldiers were called rooi-batches or red-coats for the reason that they wore red coats. The only troops on Majuba who wore khaki were the Gordons, who had come straight from the war in Afghanistan, where, for the first time, khaki was worn, the troops boiling their white linen jackets in tea leaves and then wearing them over their red coats, so as not to be so conspicuous.'

My Grandfather

BY JOHN MCNEILLIE, AUTHOR OF *WIGTOWN PLOUGHMAN*

Whether you meet him 'at the back of a hill' counting ewes, or bidding at the market, he will be wearing a heavy suit of grey-green tweeds, the material of which has been woven from the wool of his own sheep. He is a huge man with an unruly white beard and you must look for him among the oldest farmers in the Machars of Wigtownshire.

… When I was three years old, he measured me from the sole of my foot to the knee joint, as they measure horses, I believe, and he said then that I would grow to be six feet tall. I stand five feet eleven and three-quarter inches. He believes in cow dung as a healer, and fortifies his old-fashioned beliefs by first pouring Lysol into a cut. Once, while playing in a barn, I trod on the rusted prongs of a fork hidden in some straw. The horse-doctor was visiting us at the time, and my grandfather instructed him to remove the rust, and perhaps infected flesh, in order that I might be saved from the danger of lockjaw. The horse-doctor did the job with a razor, while I was firmly clamped between my grandfather's knees, and told to keep quiet, or he would 'bumph my backside'. I kept quiet – only a wean would have cried.

EPISTLES FROM AN OLD HOMESTEAD
BY HUMPHREY JOHN

A casual but excessively inbred voice from a piece of furniture informed me the other night that two million cars were licensed this Easter. Not long since this announcement would have filled me with depression at the thought of the congestion and the danger and the destruction of the quiet of the country that this increase must mean: but I was glad. I know there are people who regard the cheap car as a menace, the invasion of a privilege … and I can remember a schoolmaster saying that the motor car would do more to spread Socialism (by which he implied a mixture of Communism and Anarchy) than any other factor. Events have curiously belied his sour prophecy, since the small car has engendered an easy, widespread capitalism: for a car is a thing, like a wife or a toothbrush, of which a man does not readily share the ownership: though some constraint impels him to use it to give pleasure to other people as his guests: in which case the toothbrush part of the metaphor breaks down. These two million cars must mean that several times that number of people are able to see their goodly heritage, and to know their England in a way not otherwise possible, intimately and broadly.

The Diary of a Fruit Farmer

MAR. 21, 1939

A subscriber, writing from Cairo, states that since the building of the Assouan Dam there are no crocodiles in Egypt, so my tale of the reptile within the hen's egg is only a good story.

JUNE 22, 1939

Talking of the Malvern water, which is said to originate in Norway, a friend tells me that a water bore on the North Downs near Maidstone struck a tremendous flow which analysis proved had last seen daylight in the Himalayas. A subterranean water map would be a most fascinating possession.

OCT. 12, 1939

Read of how a rook, electrocuted as it settled on a pylon, fell in flames and set fire to a sheep. My brother when in India used in the early morning to see cranes light on the power wires, stretch up their wings to dry in the sun, make contact with the wire above, and meet with death and cremation.

NOV. 8, 1939

The New Forest ponies, painted with white stripes to look like zebras in the black-out, are objected to by their unpainted fellow ponies. This is odd, for a stuffed imitation of a calf is the normal appendage of the byre in India for stimulating the cow to part with her milk. Also a ewe will accept a strange lamb if wrapped in the skin of her dead offspring.

1940

Strength and Stay

'It would be of great help just now to many of your 21,000 fellow-readers of The Countryman *if you could very kindly say what book or books (old or new), or what study, pursuit, recreation, practice or habit of mind you have found most efficacious in yielding you refreshment at this time.'* So we wrote at the end of October to a number of our readers of different callings, responsibilities, interests and experience. Here are some representative replies with which we have been favoured …

R.D. BLUMENFELD,
Chairman, 'Daily Express'
When I can't get from the radio what I need I turn for my lighter entertainment to the Continental stations controlled by Germany: their bulletins are extremely funny provided you do not give way to impatience at their criminal intent.

LORD COCHRANE OF CULTS
At three-score years and ten, after a varied career in the Army, the House of Commons, and in business, I took up farming as a serious occupation. I have been enjoying this life now for twelve years. When the War broke out I said that now, in spite of my age, I could still do something to help my country. A few days ago I walked up a hill to inspect a 50-acre field of old grass being ploughed for wheat. While thus engaged, my attention was drawn to booming sounds from the direction of

the Forth Bridge – the German attack. On my way home I walked through a field where some of my beautiful cows were lying peacefully in the gleams of autumn sunshine. I walked near to one which gazed placidly at me with gentle eyes. I said 'Hitler' to her sharply. She just winked one eye, lazily brushed an imaginary fly with her tail and went on chewing the cud. I have no doubt farming is most efficacious in yielding me refreshment at this time.

ERIC KENNINGTON, *Artist*
Building sheds for carts, trailers and bikes, repairing gates, wire, etc., and sticking to the earth on all fours.

MAJOR-GENERAL
L.C. DUNSTERVILLE, C.M.G.,
the original of Rudyard Kipling's 'Stalky'
In retirement and at my advanced age I act as far as may be possible on the instructions given in the Laws

of Brahma, 'When a householder is advanced in years, when he perceives his skin become wrinkled, he should disengage himself from all business ties and repair to a lonely wood.' I withdraw from all active participation in the affairs of the community and content myself with philosophic contemplation of the strivers of whom I was once one ... I am still healthy and active and I dare say there are many things I could do with great interest and general efficiency, but I cannot think of any official occupation in which I would not feel I was displacing some younger man. I have had my turn and do not wish to stand in the way of others whose skin is not yet wrinkled.

THE RT. HON. C.R. ATTLEE, M.P., *Leader of the Opposition*

Briefly, I find the best occupation in vigorous forms of manual work; and for books, preferably English classics – Jane Austen is very soothing.

THE HON. SIR STAFFORD CRIPPS, K.C., M.P.

Nothing except trying to think and work out some method by which we may get a better and saner world after the tragedy is over.

> *There were a stranger in the pub, and down 'e sets and takes off 'es boot and 'es sock and puts 'es big toe in 'es mouth. 'Now then, Fatty,' says 'e to me, 'thee cean't do that.' Now I knowed as 'e 'ad me there, but I says to un, 'Oh,' I says, 'that's nothen,' I says; 'I got a babby a' whoam as can do that, an' better'n thee!'*

EPISTLES FROM AN OLD HOMESTEAD

THE INGENUOUS EVACUEE AND OTHER MATTERS
BY SOLOMON WISEACRE

When, precisely four years ago, I handed over the Epistle from my Old Homestead to Humphrey John in his, could anything have seemed less likely, Sir, than that after his 1914–1918 in France, he should, by 1939, be serving again? If, in grimmer times than those in which we enjoyed his Montaigne-like quality, I am brought back to your pages, I may be excused if this quarter I strike a graver note than his. What is wrong with the world that this should be the third Franco-German War in my life-time?

I was interested in what you told me that, in preparing this issue, you had originally planned to exclude all allusion to the War, to exclude even the word. At first, I thought you were right. On consideration, I am glad that you did not feel free to act in this way … I believe that your subscribers would have found it unworthy in their *Countryman* had it come out with a pretence that nothing of supreme importance was happening in the world. A walled-in, Jane Austen or Gilbert White-like view of Rural Britain, or a forced forgetfulness, would have contented none of us.

You will want my evacuee stories. (How quickly the accent has come off in our hospitable language!) I can tell of a woman [who], invited to help with her cottager hostess's washing, explained, as a person with a certain standing in society, that she never did her own. Gave it to a poor neighbour, to help her out. Helped her out in this way. Having done the washing, the poor neighbour pawned it until the end of the week, when, with her man's money in her hand, she redeemed it and returned it to the owner.

… As for the stories I have heard of East and South London 'randy wives', of fleas and other active humble life, and of the trooping back to Slumdom, I remain firmly persuaded that the descent of even the most outrageous strangers and the company they brought have been one of the best things that have happened to the countryside. All the grades of rural society – seven, or perhaps eight, I think, in our parts – have had a wholesome reminder of the existence of an Urban Britain of which they had no realizing sense. Some of them had pretended it was not there. Well they have seen it now; have felt it, some of them.

The shadow of war drifting over the village (January 1940), from Richard Church's Calling for a Spade.

A Fruit Grower's Diary
by Raymond Bush

FEB. 26, 1940

A little evacuee girl told her farmer host it was no wonder the old sow was so big, with ten little pigs busy blowing her up.

JUNE 2, 1940

Passed, in a train, a field where, on just such another Sunday afternoon some years ago, I saw a man in a black suit and a bowler hat walking along a path. Behind him, charging head down, was a large bull. The train roared on and I never saw or heard the end of the tale.

AUG. 2, 1940

My mother at eighty-four has produced two superb tomato plants in pots. I have advised her to give up smoking since in the "R.H.S. Journal" it is stated that a severe infection of tobacco mosaic disease can be, and is, readily transmitted to the tomato if tended by tobacco and cigarette addicts.

AUG. 31, 1940

Our dugout much in use. We have seen planes fall in flames, parachutes open and sail slowly down; and to-day a pilot came to tea who before lunch had hurtled head foremost into a whole squadron of bombers. For the modern youth space and time have ceased to exist.

SEPT. 8, 1940

Measured a bomb crater (one of six) in a Hampshire corn field; it was 39ft across and 13ft deep. Owner is delighted, having always wanted a pond there but fearing the cost of excavating the heavy gault clay.

SEPT. 18, 1940

'You look cold, child,' said the kind lady to the little Cockney evacuee; 'what clothes have you got on?' 'Coif; petty-coif; Dicky-cum-bobs; shimmy-doodle; then Oi!' was the somewhat disconcerting answer.

SEPT. 28, 1940

From 'The Daily Telegraph': A farm in Yoxford, Suffolk, was sold in 1920 for £2,500; in 1927, for £15,000; in 1934, for £750; and when it changed hands again three years later it fetched only £400.

In Days to Come

BY R. QUARENDON, PH.D., B.SC.

The mineral wealth which man uses so prodigally must one day be exhausted, whereas plant and animal life can ensure a supply of materials year after year so long as the sun continues to shine. Will manufacturers of the future, then, come to rely on the farmer for their raw materials?

In America millions of pounds are being spent on research into new ways of utilizing farm products; four State-financed laboratories have been established, and privately-endowed foundations and private firms are also at work. In this country the Potato Marketing Board has plans to set up factories for the utilization of potatoes; and the Government of Eire recently started factories for making power-alcohol from the same sources. It is proposed in India to use molasses for the production of alcohol – in South Africa, maize. But alcohol can be made also from beet, apples, apricots, pineapples, straw, nutshells, peat and wood. Remember that some 80 million tons of motor spirit disappear into the air every year.

Agriculture is still the world's greatest industry. The farmer already supplies a third, in terms of value, of all raw materials used in manufacture, to the tune of £25,000,000,000 a year; and it is the aim of chemurgy, which is the newly coined name for this new department of science, to find a use for the world's surplus farm produce as well as for the crops specially grown for manufacturers. The 'Farm Chemurgic Journal' was started in 1938.

It is the inexhaustibility of living matter which is the attraction of the farm to the far-seeing industrialist as a source of raw materials. For such unlikely things as steel, glass, aluminium and bricks the farmer and the chemist between them can produce substitutes. Plastics are being used instead of metal where strength, lightness and durability are required. They can be made exclusively from farm products, and often more cheaply. The soya bean, the amazing crop made famous by Henry Ford, will be, many farm economists believe, the mainstay of the manufacturing front. Experiments in Oxfordshire and Lincolnshire have resulted in a company being formed for its cultivation on a commercial scale in this country. It furnishes synthetic resin, plastics, paints, enamels, varnishes, linoleum, soap, margarine, glycerine, inks, glues, explosives, fertilizers and medicines, besides being an excellent cattle feed.

Casein fibre comes from milk and is said to be easier to dye than natural wool. Casein plastics are made in large quantities. There are also casein adhesives; while recently a transparent rubber has been added to the list. Large sums are being spent to find other uses for milk, and a factory has started to produce a protein known as zein from corn, which forms a valuable raw material for the manufacture of plastics, for printing inks and paper-finishing. Plastics from coffee open up an enormous new field for Brazilian planters.

... Oils, pectins for jam-making and citric acid are being made from unsaleable fruit. In Palestine oranges will soon form the raw material in the production of solvents for the manufacture of paint, varnish and synthetic rubber. That Australian pest, the prickly pear, yields a good quality illuminating gas; an Indian weed, the water hyacinth, can be processed to give motor spirit and a fertilizer. We think of motor cars usually in terms of metal; but it has been estimated that a million motor cars require 3,000,000lb of wool from 800,000 sheep, 90,000,000lb of cotton, 2,500,000lb of linseed oil, 500,000 bushels of maize, 300,000lb of mohair and 1,000,000lb of lard as well.

1941

Business Man into Farmer

... To a city man perhaps the greatest contrast between town and country life is in the interest people take in one another. When I was a sales manager no one showed concern about my work except my board. I had no hope of walking down the street and meeting someone keen to know how my sales were going. In fact, practically no one knew what my job was. In the country everyone is interested in everything I am doing. 'How did you get on with that cow you bought last week?' or 'What kind of a crop did you thresh out?' and of course I am equally interested in their activities. We all care about that absorbing subject, the weather. We don't grumble because it rains, or groan about the heat. Weather is a live topic of conversation because its changes affect our livelihood.

J.B.T.

THE VERNACULAR – RADNORSHIRE

In Radnorshire there is the peculiar form of the interrogative verb, 'Bista tired?' 'Canna', 'binna', 'costa', 'dosta' are other forms in common use. Then there are uncommon names. 'Apishtie' is a young sheep-dog; 'gullies' are newly-hatched ducklings, 'oolerts' owls, 'goleenies' game-fowl, 'rooters' pigs, and 'oonts' moles. 'Whitty-berries' are the fruit of the mountain-ash, alders 'orles', and sloes 'slans'. A steep bit of road is a 'pitch', a small rounded hill a 'tump'. The house-wife stirs her jam with a 'mundle', and will make in her 'steen' a 'turn-out-naked' or suet-pudding. 'Suppin' is bread and milk and oatmeal, and the youngsters may be 'push-along' for lunch. She 'rids up' her hearth, 'poons' her mats, 'dunches' her linen in the tub, sends her shoes to be 'tapped' or resoled, and 'douts' her candle.

The children may help to make hay with the 'pikle', and ride home on the 'gambo'; they may go 'blackberry-anting' or 'wimberry-scrattin', 'guddle' for trout in the 'prills', search for mushrooms in the 'bylets', or go to school along the 'sidelant piece', a footpath round the shoulder of a hill. People who give up readily are said to be 'easy donked', a servile person is 'slike', and it is 'nextway' to give a visitor nothing but 'boughten' cake. A sulky or shame-faced lad is said to wear a 'killship' look; an ill-tempered woman is 'whiney-peevey', and a delicate person 'nesh'. Work ill-done is said to be 'kaimet', and the person responsible is 'ran-dan'.

E.M.J.

A Fruit Grower's Diary
by Raymond Bush

Sept. 2, 1940

Heard the strange tale of the maggot king who breeds gentles for fishermen and for hospitals, where in many cases they are preferred to leeches. This man hangs carrion about the countryside to attract flies and thus gets new blood for his industry. As many as thirty dead cows go to his farm in a week.

Sept. 24, 1940

Rose hips are now hailed as the greatest source of vitamin C. This is no new discovery. As a schoolboy, 45 years ago, I had noted the amazing increase in activity which followed when a pinch of the dried internal fibre of the hip was dropped in the form-master's hat. We knew it then as Russian fleas.

NOT SO DULL IN THE COUNTRY
BY A SUFFOLK FARMER

Dec. 12. Some months ago C. bought hundreds of mouse traps as a speculation, and has sold them to the Army for use as paper clips.

Town and country rubbed up against each other during the war when land girls came on to the farms, and the advertisers were quick to spot a good opportunity.

The Land Girl's Song

I'm milking – at last I can actually milk
It took me some time, but I stuck it
So now I milk Buttercup, Daisy and Jane
And I really get froth on the bucket!
I think by next week I shall even milk four.

My word, we are
Winning the War!

I'm feeding the calves and the pigs and the hens
(Yes, I carefully boil all the swill)
And the cows and the horses, the sheep and the ducks
Oh, the coupons are tiresome, but still
The hens go on laying, the pigs are eight score

My word, we are
Winning the War!

I'm hoeing, my word I should say I can hoe
I've been doing it for weeks and for weeks
My back's used to stooping, but how I do wish
That my blouse wouldn't gap from by breeks!
But the crops are all growing as never before
So what matter – we're Winning the War!

I'm ploughing, my word, I should say I can plough.
The tractor is always my choice.
I have dragged, drilled and harrowed,
* disc-harrowed and all*
And I sing at the top of my voice
As I swing round the headland and turn up once
* more*
'My word, we are Winning the War!'

'Cavesson.'

False Tongue

Now I'll tell 'ee zummat. We 'ad a might gurt cart'oss one time and she were a proper terror. Nobody dursn't go near thic 'oss. 'Arness 'er? It took a brave man to go handy'er and say 'Good marning' pleasant, let alone tark 'bout 'arness. But I could go near 'er. Ho yes! There warn't no kicking nor biting nor nothing o' that when I did go to groom 'er, she did bide quiet as a lamb, and no matter what I did tell thic 'oss to do, she done it pretty smartish. And I'll tell 'ee how that were. I 'ad zummat in me pocket – in me westkit pocket 'ere, as 'ee might 'ave thee watch or anything o' that, an' I'll bet thee a pound to a shillin' 'ee dusn' know what I 'ad in me pocket. I 'ad a valse tongue in me pocket. That's what I 'ad. A valse tongue. And I'll tell 'ee what valse tongue is. Every foal that's born 'as two tongues, an' one o' them's a valse tongue, and as soon as a foal's born 'e shakes 'is 'ead and zummat drops out of 'is mouth. Then 'ee must dart forrard main smart an' pick it up. That's a valse tongue, and you've got to nip in quick to get it else the mare'll eat it. An' if 'ee do dry thic valse tongue an' put un in yer pocket and stand handy a hoss so's 'e do get the smell of it, 'ee can do what 'ee likes to hoss or mare an' no matter whether the 'oss is a kicker or a biter or anything 'ee likes to mention, as sure as thic 'ere 'alter's in me 'and, that 'oss'll do anythin' thee tells 'im.

M.H.R-M.

[The false tongue, second tongue or hippomanes, is a small spatulate object, 3 to 6in long and half as broad, brownish in colour. It has much the consistency of a tongue. It is found, not in the foal's mouth, but loose inside the foetal membranes, and usually slips out when the foal is born. Fleming's 'Veterinary Obstetrics' says that it is probably the coagulated solids from the foetal urine, which is passed into the allantoic fluid. Some old carters are keen to obtain this object; they are also secretive as to why they want it. Mares, like other animals, are always interested in their foetal membranes, eating them if they can, and it is possible that the faintly foetal odour hanging round the false tongue would occupy the mare's attention while she was harnessed, etc. *J.W.R.S.*]

> '*Heard about the land girl? When she went into the milking shed first she said, "Can I start on a calf? I'm a bit afraid of cows".*'

As It Seems to Some of Us

The charge of eating song-birds

Our American subscribers will be pleased to know that the stories in some of their papers that our people are so hard put to it that they have taken to eating song-birds, crows and sparrows, are exaggerated. We learn that there were advertisements in some Irish papers for song-birds for export to London, but the attention of the Eire police was called to the illegality of such a traffic and the advertisements ceased to appear. The secretary and several members of the Royal Society for the Protection of Birds who visited poulterers' shops have been unable to find larks for sale.

A Fruit Grower's Diary

by Raymond Bush

May 31, 1942

Last night my third grand-daughter arrived, heralded by the siren blowing the 'All Clear'. My daughter (her mother) was born on the night of the first Zeppelin raid in the last War and has been Zeppy to us ever since. As a great believer in the natural feeding of infants she says, 'It seems to me a good idea since it doesn't go sour overnight and it's where the cat can't get at it.'

June 1, 1942

Two cows, Buttercup and Daisy, were exchanging confidences over the boundary hedge. 'And how do you find your new milker?' 'Oh not so bad; a bit slow, but then he was a hairdresser before the War. How is your new man shaping?' 'Terrible; he was the bellringer in the parish church until he took to milking.'

Sept. 16, 1942

An Australian standing by the hotel window, looking out on the barrage balloons as they strained at their moorings in the pouring rain, shrugged his shoulders and turned away remarking, 'Beats me why they don't cut the cables and let the derned island sink.'

Introducing Britain

A copy of those entertaining and wholly admirable instructions to men in the United States Services on how things are in this country and how Americans should order themselves with their British acquaintances has come our way. They are contained in seven mimeographed, closely-typed foolscap pages. We extract passages about the countryside.

England is smaller than North Carolina or Iowa. The whole of Great Britain – that is England, Scotland and Wales together – is hardly bigger than Minnesota. England's largest river, the Thames (pronounced 'Tems') is not even as big as the Mississippi when it leaves Minnesota. No part of England is more than one hundred miles from the sea.

If you are from Boston or Seattle the weather may remind you of home. If you are from Arizona or North Dakota you will find it a little hard to get used to. At first you will probably not like the almost continual rains and mists and the absence of snow and crisp cold. Actually, the city of London has less rain for the whole year than many places in the United States, but the rain falls in frequent drizzles. Most people get used to the English climate eventually.

If you have a chance to travel about you will agree that no area of the same size in the United States has such a variety of scenery. At one end of the English channel there is a coast like that of Maine. At the other end are the great white chalk cliffs of Dover. The lands of South England and the Thames valley are like farm or grazing lands of the eastern United States, while the lake country in the north of England and the highlands of Scotland are like the White Mountains of New Hampshire. In the east, where England bulges out toward Holland, the land is almost Dutch in appearance, low, flat and marshy. The great wild moors of Yorkshire in the north and Devon in the south-west will remind you of the Badlands of Dakota and Montana.

Britain may look a little shop-worn to you. There's been a war on since 1939. The houses haven't been painted because factories are not making paint – they're making 'planes. The famous English gardens and parks are either unkempt because there are no men to take care of them, or they are being used to grow needed vegetables. The trains are unwashed and grimy because men and women are needed for more important work than car-washing. The British people are anxious for you to know that in normal times Britain looks much prettier, cleaner, neater.

You will have difficulty with some of the local dialects, and it may comfort you to know that a farmer or villager from Cornwall very often can't understand a farmer or villager in Yorkshire or Lancashire. But you will learn.

1943

Murrain

Foot-and-mouth disease has broken out at —— in ——shire. – B.B.C.

No cows graze in Housepiece; no calves scamper in the Little Mead. The yearlings have ceased to call from the hill; the dry cows are gone from the moor. There are no springers in the orchard, and the bull's pen stands empty. Dead, dead, all dead. They have slaughtered Daisy, slaughtered Fidget, Marigold and Tulip, Buttercup and Rose.

The mornings are silent, deathly silent. There is no scuffle of hooves, no lowing of cows, no blaring of calves, no clanking of chains. No churns clatter, no pails ring, there is no hum from the milking machine, no hiss and rattle from the sterilizer. The milking pens are empty, the dairy herd is dead. Pansy and Patience, Cherry and Dinah, Ladybird and Plum – all, all are gone.

I had reared them and bred them, milked them and fed them, groomed and clipped, poulticed and drenched them. But only the mice go to the hay-mow and rats to the corn-bin. The kale stands in the field uncut; the mangold clamp is unopened. For the beasts are gone; the byres are empty. Only the wind rattles the barn door, only the sparrows chatter in the yard. Princess was slaughtered, Snowball was slaughtered, Tiny and Nigger, Beautiful and Nell.

I had loved them and cursed them, the good old ladies, the contrary bitches, the comical toads, my pretty little cows. They were my taskmasters and my servants, my occupation and my livelihood, my ambition and my endless chore. Mermaid and Bluebell, Fidelity and Dainty, Hollyhock and Pearl. Dead, all dead.

I lean from my window dreaming I see in the moon's dark shadows those quiet forms lying placid, content beneath the hedgerow. But morning dawns on deserted meadows, on empty stalls, on silent yards. For my daily companions have all been slaughtered, my kindly friends have been buried in lime. And I walk sadly across the barton, awaiting the day when I shall welcome another Nancy, a new Blackbird, Cowslip and Topsy, Jubilee and Star. *U.D.*

" A dear old lady fresh from the local sewing bee had heard the reason of the onion shortage. The Government needed all the onions to make tear gas. " Raymond Bush

1944

Wild Life and Tame

THE WAY OF A VIXEN

My father felled a vixen which his dog had trapped, threw it into an outhouse, and secured the door. After breakfast he slung it over his shoulder and started for the keeper's house, two miles across the moor. About half-way there he threw down the vixen, lit his pipe, gazed round for a few minutes, picked up the vixen and proceeded. When half a mile from his destination, he had to climb a six-foot wall, so he threw the vixen over first. When he reached the other side it had gone! J.McC.
[The vixen was probably 'playing possum' – a ruse that is rare among the higher animals, though well known among foxes. When insects feign death, their actions may be regarded as purely instinctive, but it seems likely that the wily fox acts deliberately, and that it has at least a partial understanding of the purpose of the game it is playing. R.M.]

"*Holding a rooster by the wings, the little girl from town was upbraiding him for bad manners. 'Why, Jeannie, whatever are you doing?' asked the farmer's wife. 'Well, I've been watching him. He's very rude. He eats the food and never goes into the nest to lay an egg.' 'But cockerels don't lay, dear.' 'Then why do you keep them?'*"

Hints for the Home Acre

BY FRANK S. STUART

ADVENTURE WITH BEES

… Came the task of moving the bees. Usually, the owners would not sell the hives, only the contents … Once, going round a corner on a steep downhill with two hives, one hive half fell out, and the top dropped off, letting thousands of bees fly fiercely up. The other hive jammed across the hand-brake, so that I could not click it on to hold the car. There I sat, unveiled and in shirt sleeves, mobbed by angry bees. I could keep the car at a standstill only so long as my foot was on the foot-brake; any sudden move would precipitate both hives on to the road. Incidentally, to get two hives into an Austin Seven, you have to take out all seats and cushions and sit on the floor to drive. I edged the car into the bank, which held it still, and then got out and tackled those bees. I could not get them back, but I got the hives in place and most of the bees clung on outside the hive, complaining, or came to sting me. (When you have enough bee-stings – some hundreds – you become relatively immune, and a sting has no more effect than a nettle-prick.) …

COUNTRYMAN CLUB

FROM THE FRENCH

Besides 'ashet' (assiette) you hear in Scotland 'grosars' (gooseberries) and 'manty' (dressmaker) which we assume were brought over by Mary Queen of Scots. – S.A. I have read of, but never heard used, the call to cows 'prichidam' (approchez, mesdames). – E.P.

MORE OLD NAMES

… The name of a hamlet, not far from Newcastle-on-Tyne, called Pity Me, comes from 'Petite Mer', which some French prisoners called a sheet of water in the vicinity. By the Roman Wall there is an artillery practice camp near an old Roman camp which the Romans named Ad Fines, as it appeared to them to be at the end of everything. The British gunners who go up into that barren spot give it a similar distinction by calling it 'the bloody limit'. – Colonel

CUTE

An American pilot who has done a lot of flying up and down our valley recently told someone that he thought it was cute the way we had camouflaged the village. It turned out that he was referring to the many thatched houses. – H.U.

A Fruit Grower's Diary
by Raymond Bush

JAN. 11, 1944

Starlings (revolting diet!) are being advertised in 'Brighton as 'special' at three for 2s 0d.

MAY 12, 1944

Six cows were penned in a field by an electric fence. After the first shock they never went near it again until another sow was added to the company. The sows then edged her towards the wire and as she duly received her shock the six threw up their heels and scampered off delighted with their little joke. So I'm told.

MAY 16, 1944

An ex-gardener of mine won many gallons of beer over a parsnip with a root 20 feet long. It grew through brickwork and dropped down to well water. Today a Nottingham man told me of the root of an oak tree which penetrated a quarter of a mile into a coal-pit. Next!

JUNE 28, 1944

An alert was on and the sky was flecked with anti-aircraft bursts as I left the station this evening. A diminutive A.T.S. girl asked me if she could walk across the fields to the village with me. She was afraid of the cows!

JULY 4, 1944

A man of 70 has recently cycled 440 miles to Scotland in seven days, subsisting entirely on grass growing by the road-side.

AUG. 9, 1944

D.D.T., dichloro-diphenyl trichloro-ethane to the chemist, or Double Delirium Tremens as a Yankee reporter dubbed it, looks like being a useful, if selective, insecticide for the fruit grower. It is said to attack the central nervous system of fleas, flies, earwigs, wasps, some caterpillars, celery fly, apple blossom weevil and cockroaches. Yet it is no cure for greenfly.

1945

WHERE
THE CHOCOLATE GOES

... On troopships—in Naafi canteens behind the fighting zones—in every paratroop soldier's emergency rations— in every lifeboat in the Merchant Navy—on supply ships going out to Italy and the Middle East...*chocolate*. The sustaining powers of chocolate have long been officially recognized, and today four-fifths of the total output from our Bournville factory goes to Government priorities. That is why there is less Cadburys in the shops.

CADBURY
means ·
QUALITY

OUR READERS' MOTORING TALES

A main road, with two secondary roads leading right and left, and a narrow by-lane to green fields. Down the main road pours an American convoy with the latest motor weapons. From one side road jeeps follow one another like, as an old man remarks, 'wopses out of a fallen apple', guided by two military police, whose white sleeves shine in the sunlight. A double-decker bus, laden to capacity, groans up the hill, and ordinary cars and bikes in plenty pass as they can find road space. Then the bus groans to a standstill, the war machines signal dead slow, the jeeps take on the slow crawl of drunken wasps on an autumn afternoon, and the M.P.s stand at ease. Out of the narrow lane comes a small pony, harnessed to a small cart and driven by a small sturdy boy with blackberry-stained mouth. The cart contains an armful of golden wheat-straw, forming a bed for a new, very new, calf. Following the cart, her head over the tailboard, anxiety in her every movement, comes a beautiful Jersey cow, with a splendid bag. They pass to the farm and the Americans speed up, the M.P.s stand to attention, the jeeps accelerate, the bus clanks into life, while overhead a formation of silvery aeroplanes sweeps into the blue. *V.G.*

During the war, advertisers needed to remind the public of their products, and explain why they were currently unavailable – as in this Cadbury's advertisement from 1945.

" On an estate where everything was run on business-like lines, the cattle in summer lay close to the poultry-houses, and the hens had learnt to pick the flies off the eyelids and other parts of the animals. Mistress to hen-wife, 'You ought to send the grieve a bill for keeping his cattle free of flies.' 'Not I,' said the hen-wife, 'he'd send me a bill for chicken food.' "

In the Country and Out of It

'Such complete ruin is scarcely credible,' writes an American subscriber in north-western Germany. 'No single isolated peasant farm has survived from the burning. The carcases of cattle lie tethered in their stalls; the winter wheat is all ground under by the tanks. In the evening, through habit, loosed cattle go back to the places where cowhouses were and stand there and low, and there is no-one to tend them. Sometimes one of our boys who has been a farmer will milk them, and I saw two soldiers cutting up swedes for a bull. Horses wander across the landscape, the heavy draught horses apparently enjoying their freedom, for they kick up their heels like colts. Animals soon disregard artillery fire, and cows will graze within a few feet of cows that have been killed and pay no attention at all.' This reached me at the beginning of April.

" Village War crosses serve no useful purpose. Many memorials are downright ugly. They are chosen by the wrong people. Those who have to queue up in snow and rain for country and suburban buses are the class which suffers the greatest losses in any war. Well-designed, weatherproof shelters with a plain board within recalling the names of the local dead would offer grateful reminder and a permanent protection. "

Raymond Bush

1946

A HOT FAVOURITE!
THIRTY TO ONE – ON.

30 Operations with **ONE** Tractor

That is one reason why the 'Trusty' leads the field. The whole range of implements are designed to carry out any operation. The implements, when fitted, become a power-driven tool. Each can be changed in minutes; the patent swinging draw bar makes it child's play. Power steering is fitted for easy handling and manœuvreability. You supervise—the 'Trusty' does the work.

The spirit of self-sufficiency, 1946 style!

As It Seems to Some of Us
THE COLOUR OF FARM IMPLEMENTS

THE INGENIOUS AND ENJOYABLE 'Brains Trust' admits sometimes that a question has stumped it, or adventures views and is mistaken. It came a cropper, for example, on the reason why farm implements are painted particular colours. The base of the paint (generally a good lead paint) is more important than the colour pigment, though some blues and greens tend to lose their colour more quickly than, say, red. Most manufacturers rely on the colour of their paint to identify and advertise their products. Thus David Brown, International and Massey-Harris tractors and implements are red, Ransomes blue, Case and Allis Chalmers orange, M.M. yellow, Oliver green, Ford-Ferguson grey, etc.

Doctoring in Horse-and-Trap Days

BY HARRY ROBERTS

My first medical practice was in the little village-town of Hayle in Cornwall, where I lived for nearly ten years at the end of the last century. I paid three hundred pounds for it, without seeing it; indeed I bought it by wire. Then I got myself a smallish cob, sound and well-broken, together with a dog cart and harness.

… Except on Sunday morning, one rarely saw a Cornishman walking any distance. Anything more than a mile was covered by bicycle or donkey-cart; and every married man expected his wife to bring to his place of work, at midday, a hot Cornish pasty wrapped in a clean white cloth. In money matters they were very honest and self-respecting. They paid – in relation to their financial status – high fees, and they never grudged paying bills of many pounds for treatment for a sick child, but they liked to get the skill and attention they paid for.

… An old doctor, my nearest fellow practitioner, when called at night to a confinement at some distance, would, if he found that things were not moving very quickly, have his horse taken out and stabled, and would himself remove his boots and coat and get into bed beside the patient. Here, after telling the nurse in charge to wake him when there was anything doing, he would finish his night's sleep in peace.

WILD ELEPHANTS

I HAVE SPENT YEARS inventing means to exclude wild elephants from young rubber clearings in India. Five miles of 6 by 4 ft trench with a 5 ft high wire fence did not deter them, but when the gigantic corner posts they had uprooted were replaced by slender pieces of bamboo, they left these alone. I have watched them making 'slippery-slides' down a steep slope and teaching their young the sport of tobogganing. They form an almost continuous line from terminus to starting-point, stopping occasionally to seize a young rubber plant with which to chastise a recalcitrant and shrieking 'baby'.

Major John Wilson

1947–1957

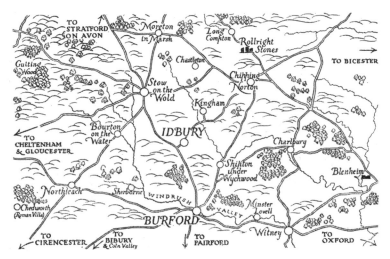

Rebuilding the Countryside

I n 1947, at the age of 80, the founder of *The Countryman* decided to step down as editor after 20 years in the job, though he continued for many years to contribute to its pages and take an active interest in its affairs. The new editor, John Cripps, was the son of an old friend, Sir Stafford Cripps, and would remain in the role for even longer than R.S. – right through to 1971. Thus he saw the journal through the years of rebuilding the countryside after the war and into a period of optimism and prosperity – and beyond into the time when the rapid growth of agribusiness began to be questioned by some.

With the new editorship came a change of premises: the journal moved out of Robertson Scott's home at Idbury and into Sheep Street, Burford, a few ambling miles down the road. This would be its editorial home for the next 50 years. In the spring of 1957 the price would increase for the first time,

(Above) On 1st April 1947 the offices of The Countryman *moved from the founder editor's home at Idbury to the small town of Burford, five miles away. This helpful map was printed in the Spring issue.*

to three shillings an issue, and in the same year the cover would be illustrated for the first time, with one of the line drawings for which the journal was already well known.

Meanwhile agriculture was advancing apace after the war and huge investments led to great increases in production – though perhaps without enough thought for animal welfare, wildlife and the landscape. Intensive farming of pigs and poultry, for example, became widespread; the horse was finally ousted from its role on the farm; machines ousted human workforces from the fields (there were 3,000 combines in 1946 and this more than trebled to 10,000 by 1950 and trebled again to 31,000 by 1956); and new buildings on the farm were built from factory materials such as concrete, steel, asbestos, corrugated iron and plastic rather than local bricks and stone and oak.

The old landowners were quickly vanishing, and along with them their sense of duty to the community. The new landowners had little time or thought for their own parish folk, but the farm workers and villagers were no longer subdued into putting up with poor conditions. There were plenty of urban jobs for those who found that farm work did not pay well enough; and women in the villages were not afraid to demand better domestic standards for their families. More and more families had cars, which meant villagers could travel more easily for their work and their holidays; it also meant that a lot more people from the towns could come and sample the delights of the countryside, either as tourists or as commuters.

The Town and Country Planning Act of 1947 reflected a new attitude to building, and was a major talking point in the columns of *The Countryman*, whose pages also fizzed with talk of national parks and nature reserves and, yet again, conflicting views on fox hunting. Wildlife continued to be a subject of great interest, and it was in this period that the naturalist Bruce Campbell became a regular part of the team. Another topic was the building of village halls, many of which were memorials to those who had died during the war.

At the start of the period, rationing was still in force; in fact bread was rationed for the first time in July 1946. A few years later country dwellers were faced with the ugliness of myxomatosis in rabbits: the disease wiped out 99 per cent of the rabbit population and their lingering deaths with bulging blind eyes exploding from their heads turned the countryside into a living nightmare. But it was also during this period, during the 1950s, that the nation celebrated the coronation of Queen Elizabeth II and enjoyed the great Festival of Britain. Life was definitely getting better.

A Farmer's Ruminations

BY CLYDE HIGGS

As a landowner, I welcome the Town and Country Planning Bill; far too much of our countryside has been ravaged already by indiscriminate building, and anything that will ensure the proper utilization of land will be well received by most people, if not by a farmer in a nearby village who has just completed selling a frontage that cost him £30 an acre at £450, and was happily starting on the other side of the road. I wonder how much the paper value of my estate has declined.

… The report of the Committee on Footpaths and Access to the Countryside may appeal to town-dwellers who like to feel that they can enjoy at will the freedom of the countryside without responsibilities, but footpaths across or round cultivated land, either grass or arable, may be a nuisance to the farmer. It is recommended that these paths should be established on a permanent basis for a purpose for which they were not always intended. They originated when Shanks's mare was the usual conveyance and every yard counted.

They were never designed as hikers' highways. My farm is intersected by many paths, which often cross fields diagonally. Surely a slight detour would add to the walkers' pleasure, and it would allow me to cultivate my land efficiently. Some hikers have little knowledge of the countryside and disregard the golden rule to leave gates as they are found. Often our Monday morning job is to sort out the mix-up.

A little note from John A. Stevenson about the use of aircraft in agriculture in British Columbia included an American cartoon from 'Wallace's Farmer' with a novel method of harvesting.

ANSWERS TO CORRESPONDENTS

WHAT'S IN A SPIDER?

FINDING A DEAD SPIDER, I threw it on the fire. It did not flare up and disintegrate, but remained intact; even some of its legs, sticking out quite unsupported, were unaffected by the heat. After 25 minutes I carefully removed it with an old spoon, and, examining it under a lens, found that even the minute hairs on the legs were intact. This suggests that the bulk of the spider consists of mineral matter, probably calcium phosphate and/or carbonate, or alternatively silica or some siliceous compound. The body and legs were blackened, probably due to carbon, but retained their shape.

T.H. Byrom, F.I.C., Bushey, Herts

COUNTRYMAN CLUB

SUDDEN DEATH

I can pass on the culinary secret of Rebecca to which Elizabeth Keith refers (Spring 1947). I learned it in Portuguese East Africa, where the staple meat course, in those days, was the inevitable chicken, locally termed 'cuckoo'. When called on to provide a meal for an unexpected guest, the boy was said to give the bird a teaspoonful of whisky, with the result that, although it would be killed and cooked for immediate consumption, the flesh was always tender! – *Joseph Pyke*. * In Ceylon, a few small pieces of an unripe papaw are put with the bird before cooking. This does not affect the taste of the dish, but the milky juice of the fruit makes the meat tender by means of a ferment which it contains. – *S.K. Wallooppillai*

" *Mark Twain wrote: 'To cease smoking is the easiest thing I ever did. I ought to know because I have done it thousands of times.'* "

" *The first question asked in a quiz competition at a Kent village meeting was, 'How do you start your day?' A cowman said simply, 'Turn out the oil-lamp in my cottage and switch on the electric light in the cow-shed.'* "

How Fares Sweet Alderney?

BY R.M. LOCKLEY

An islandman asked the question in the train from Southampton afterwards, and there was a wistful stare upon his old sea-wrinkled face. I understood that question to its full depth. The first part of my reply made him smile with pride. 'It is a most beautiful island,' I said, and then I saw his look change to a puzzled resignation as I added, 'but sweet Alderney fares ill.' And the reason is plain.

In 1940 the fifteen hundred inhabitants were asked and agreed to leave at a moment's notice. Apart from one farmer who remained behind to 'guard' the cattle, the people were all evacuated. No-one was left to occupy and try to save houses, farms and property, as on Jersey, Guernsey and Sark (where in consequence comparatively little damage was done). The Germans used Alderney as a penitentiary for undesirable Russian prisoners. With this slave labour they built elaborate concrete fortifications and even more wonderful funk-hole warrens. They levelled the little fields of the islanders, destroying the boundary marks. They gutted houses by tearing out for firewood the floors, doors and rafters, and they burnt or exported the furniture.

When less than a fifth of the inhabitants returned in 1945 they found a heart-breaking task before them. All that was left of their prosperous agriculture was a small herd of alien cows, a bunch of gone-wild horses, and a flock of sheep. The land was pitted with trenches and holes leading to the underground labyrinth. Everywhere were the graves of unknown Russian soldiers. Alderney was a wilderness whose 'glades confess the tyrant's power'.

Yet, so strong is the love of home in the true Aldernese that this advance guard set to work willingly, and under the stewardship of Judge French repairs are now going ahead. It was agreed to issue to every re-occupied house an equal share in salvaged furniture and all new goods imported from Britain. Alderney is part of the Bailiwick of Guernsey, which promised some of its famous cattle. The farmers have agreed to work the island on a communal basis at present, each man to draw a subsistence wage of only £3 per week, until such time as the land can be reapportioned as far as possible among the original occupiers. Meanwhile, because the population remains so small and because it has not been possible to get the tourist and vegetable trades re-established, communications have been neglected.

There is, or was, no regular steamship service, and if it were not for the occasional planes calling there the inhabitants would be cruelly isolated – cruelly because, remembering how well they fought and worked away from home during the war, one feels that they are at present poorly rewarded.

The local plane rose through the white wisps of the morning mist over the glasshouse island of Guernsey ... A word in the pilot's ear brought a smile and a nod. Yes, he had seen the colony of large white birds on rocks off Alderney. No, it would be no trouble to inspect them ... A vast excitement held me as I recognized the gannets on Ortac ... Our cameras clicked furiously while the plane circled close, tilting in order to give us a clear view through the rain-spotted windows. Then we levelled out and made for the air-strip of Alderney.

A man with a wheelbarrow welcomed us with cheerful informality, and trundled our bags over the buttercups to the single island taxi, which bounced up ten minutes later

---

As It Seems to Some of Us
THE ROYAL ENGAGEMENT

THIS IS THE first occasion we have had to offer our congratulations and good wishes to Princess Elizabeth and her future Consort, who, at Gordonstoun in Morayshire, had unusual opportunities to learn to appreciate the country-side and enjoy country pursuits. This is the school particularly associated with the County Badge scheme, a method of training which, instead of putting all the emphasis on developing the particular skills of the specialized athlete, provides a standard which any boy keeping himself reasonably fit can attain. The Silver Badge offers a standard for the more athletic, but again involves a balanced training with its 'expedition test' to show a boy's ability to rely on himself in mountains or at sea, in addition to jumping, running, javelin throwing and swimming. One who knew Lieutenant Mountbatten at school writes: 'I remember Philip as being very keen on outdoor activities, above all sailing. He became one of the most responsible boy sailors, sailed with the *Princess Louise* to Norway, and helped to take her through mine-infested seas to Aberdovey when the school was evacuated to Wales. In due course he became head boy, or "guardian". He was responsible, popular and effective, and distinguished himself as an athlete, above all as a jumper, in the inter-school competitions.'

A Fruit Grower's Diary
by Raymond Bush

JULY 9, 1947

A Norfolk lady returned home to find a car in her drive, a picnic party on her lawn and a fire in the shrubbery. Taking the number of the car, she traced it to an Acton semi-detached residence to which she drove in due course, taking a deck-chair, her lunch and plenty of picnic rubbish. As the family were out she sat on their lawn and left an equivalent litter behind.

JULY 30, 1947

An Irish town council built for its 'puir divils' six cottages with the great innovation of indoor sanitation. Later a visiting inspector found that in five cottages the plumbing had been reversed. The cistern was used for boiling mash, the lead flush pipe as a condenser, and the pan as the ultimate receptacle for potato spirit.

SEPT. 24, 1947

A countrywoman suspected of illegal dealings in eggs was found in bed by the police, 'sitting' on over 300, while another 400 were under the bed. I have often thought that a hospital patient with a persistently high temperature might be persuaded to hatch out a sitting or two.

OCT. 14, 1947

Was told a tale of a mouse which was put into cold store with the apples in September and not brought out until early May. The mouse was dead but its hair had grown a foot long. My informant described it as 'most gruesome'.

DEC. 14, 1947

Barter is all the go! A Suffolk farmer traded a hundred turkeys for a new Austin car.

DEC. 15, 1947

A four-year-old Devon boy and his two-and-a-half-year-old brother were set to collect caterpillars on the cabbage patch. When mother went to see how they were getting on, the elder boy had half a tin full of wrigglers. Junior had none in his tin, but a green trickle from each corner of his mouth supported his statement 'I eats um'. He was none the worse for it, but it is to be hoped that this will not encourage the Minister of Food to cut down the proteins still further.

On Entering Our Twenty-First Year

We heartily thank readers, in this country, in the United States and in other parts of the world, for their kind messages to The Countryman *on entering its twenty-first year. We reproduce some of the autograph letters in facsimile, and wish space permitted of our doing the same with them all.*

EARL BALDWIN

Your *Countryman* is one of the joys of my life and all through the war I sent it to the Royal Navy where it was much appreciated. It is a grand work you have done and your friends are in every corner of the world.

> *Yours always sincerely*
> *Baldwin of Bewdley*

SIR STAFFORD CRIPPS

My warmest congratulations upon what has, I believe, been a work of great value to the rural interests of our country.

I recall those first days when you and I and some others who are no longer with us sat round a table discussing the prospects of launching *The Countryman*. I was optimistic in thinking you might reach a circulation of a thousand or over; the general opinion was much more modest – about five hundred. But you showed yourself a super-optimist and spoke of ten thousand!

And now it has sailed safely all over the world and has brought happiness and interest into hundreds of thousands of lives.

It has carried with it a progressive social outlook and a true philosophy of country life, and so has helped to formulate opinions which are now resulting for the first time in a real agricultural programme for the country.

The circulation must have reached over fifty times my optimistic estimate – and how glad I am that my estimate was so bad!

RAMSAY MACDONALD

Glad to find your magazine in Cape Breton and to have had a chance of commending it. With best wishes from off the coasts of Newfoundland & Labrador.   *J.R.M.*

'*Saves a lot of explanation.*'

> *Aged villager indignantly to doctor, who has told him the pains he complains of in one of his legs may be due to old age: 'Old age be danged! T'other leg, he's the same age and he's all right!'*

1948

A Fruit Grower's Diary
by Raymond Bush

APRIL 23, 1948

While eating my lunch was harassed by the death-cries of a neighbour's pig. At the moment I was reading the Penguin translation of Homer's 'Odyssey' at the part where Eumaeus, the faithful swineherd, entertains Ulysses, unaware of his identity; 'he struck the animal with a billet of oak which he had left unsplit. The hog fell dead. They slit its throat, singed its bristles and deftly cut the carcase up.' We sometimes use the humane killer today, but the Greeks evidently had a name and a use for it a thousand years B.C.

MAY 7, 1948

Almost any woody tree will provide a rooted cutting on the tree if a flower-pot is sawn or cracked into two vertical half-sections, and clamped firmly to hold in position moss packed closely round the desired shoot. Add a little soil to the top of the moss, water once or twice a day according to the weather, and in a month there should be root enough to allow the shoot to be cut off below the pot. Early spring is a good time to try this.

COUNTRYMAN CLUB

HEAD DOWNWARDS

A squire who put up two long fences planted the posts of one head downwards (opposite to the growth of the tree) and they had more than double the life of the others.   *C.H. Perkins*

As It Seems to Some of Us

IF WHALES COULD SCREAM

THE UNIVERSITIES FEDERATION for Animal Welfare and its chairman, Major C.W. Hume, deserve every support in their efforts to hasten the development and general adoption of electrical methods of killing whales. In a lecture arranged by the Federation, Dr. Harry R. Lillie, surgeon to one of last year's Antarctic whaling fleets, gave this description of present methods:

'The killing is done cruelly and inefficiently with the Svend Foyn harpoon gun invented nearly 100 years ago. This projects a harpoon carrying 1-lb charge of black powder in a delay-action grenade head. Occasionally a whale may be killed within five minutes or even immediately, but such occurrences are few, and usually the killing takes up to an hour. In one extreme case five hours and nine harpoons were required for a mother blue whale. If we can imagine a horse having two or three explosive spears stuck into its stomach and being made to pull a butcher's lorry through the streets of London while it pours blood into the gutter, finally collapsing an hour later, we shall have an idea of the present method of killing. The gunners themselves admit that if whales could scream the industry would stop, for nobody would be able to stand it, but they have no vocal chords.'

Under existing international agreements, some thirty thousand whales are killed annually.

1949

COUNTRYMAN CLUB

EGG-FLIP

I had some eggs ready for sitting and was lamenting to an Afrikaner friend that none of my hens was broody. He advised me to get a turkey hen and give her some port wine. This would make her drunk, he said, and she would then want to sit. I did this, and the hen straight away went broody. She hatched out a fine lot of chicks to whom she was a splendid mother.

S.E. Knight, Transvaal

'Built as Hampshire people used to build three or four centuries ago'

Interior of an old Hampshire barn, illustrated by Stephen Bone in an entertaining and informative 1949 article about the discovery of death-watch beetle while he was converting the ruined barn into a home.

A Fruit Grower's Diary
by Raymond Bush

JAN. 20, 1949

In the Jamaican sun, tree growth is rapid. A gwango tree planted for shade and cattle food in 1937 is today 8 ft round the stem. A coconut produces seven branches a year, each 20 ft long, with leaves up to 4 ½ ft across. Each branch may weigh 30 lb and have a shoulder a full foot across.

JAN. 22, 1949

Labour is very temperamental. Little work will be done on a Friday — too near a Saturday; not much on Monday — too near to Sunday.

MAY 6, 1949

This is the tale of a pickpocket who felt his own pocket being picked at the races. Turning round he caught the thief, a very pretty girl. Being two of a trade they fell in love and married. A year later a fine boy was born but he had one disability, his left hand remained tightly closed and could not be opened. They visited a child specialist who tried to force the hand open and made the baby cry. The specialist then pulled out his gold watch and chain and swung the watch in front of the baby. The little fellow's eyes glistened and gradually, as the watch swung, his left hand opened and out fell the midwife's gold wedding-ring.

Gloucestershire schoolmaster, pre-1914, giving an English lesson: 'Now there's three harnts; there's the harnt the relation, there's the harnt the hemmet, and there's the harnt what harnts yer.'

Twelve-year-old Orcadian, explaining why he spent on cigarettes so much of the money he earned by accompanying his father to the fishing: 'Mon, I never could tak' tae the pipe.'

Wild Life and Tame

STRANGE RAT-CATCHER

In one of the stalls in our local market we saw a loose guinea-pig picking up and chewing the soft ends of the quills of chicken feathers, which dropped on the floor as the owner of the stall plucked some fowls. When we asked the man if he would sell the animal, he replied: 'Oh, no. I have it for keeping the rats away from the fowls.' We thought that he might be pulling our legs, until he picked up the guinea-pig, which was very tame, and showed us its ears; like those of an old-time prizefighter, they bore ample testimony of many battles. He said it fought the rats, killing some and driving away others from the place where the fowls were shut up at night.
O. Molony, Monte Estoril, Portugal

" Old carter to young mate: 'Thee goo an' git the 'os an' put en in the dung cart.' 'Which un?' 'Thic owd un; wear the owd uns out fust.' 'Well, then, thee goo an' fetch en theeself.' "

Psychology and the Bull

The farmer was escorting his Jersey bull along the lane when I met him. 'You got ter understand this psychology stuff,' he said, 'before you're fit ter 'andle bulls. You got ter treat 'em same as a schoolteacher deals with a crowd o' kids. Be firm with 'em, but never be spiteful or they'll tek it out of yer later.' 'Doesn't it need two of you to control him?' I asked. 'No, no, no,' he replied, 'that'd never do. It 'ud make 'im too proud. 'E'd feel 'e was master once 'e knew it took two men ter 'andle 'im.'   *Garth Christian*

1950

AARON'S WISH

AN OLD SHROPSHIRE COUPLE had lived a cat-and-dog life and had not spoken to each other for years. In course of time the husband fell ill and lay dying. His wife, anxious for a reconciliation before it was too late, decided to make the first advance. She went upstairs to the old man's bedside and, breaking the long, long silence, said: 'Aaron, where does thee want to be buried?' The answer came back without hesitation and in a voice full of malice: 'Atop o' thee'.

G. Mary Malcolm, Gobowen

" After watching a farm hand milk a cow, a small boy, on a visit to a dale farm from a West Riding town, touched him on the arm: 'Noo, mister, put it back and do it all ower ageean.' "

Sprats from Seed

As I was sitting in an inn in Hampshire, I overheard this conversation:

'Mornin', Jack.'

'Mornin', Bill; seen George lately?'

'Aye, I saw 'im last night.'

'Did 'e tell 'bout they seeds I give 'im?'

'No. Why?'

'Well, George asked me fer some seeds, an' I said I 'ad some which I 'adn't, so I goes an' buys some cod's roe, cooks it, separates it out, dries it 'ard, puts some in a bag and gives 'em to 'im. I saw nowt of George for a week or so. When I 'ave run into 'im I say, 'ow they seeds doing? Oh, 'e says, fine; come down tomorrow an' 'ave a look at 'em. So down I goes, and did George 'ave the laugh on me; 'e bin an' bought some sprats. And thur they was in a luvely straight line with their 'eads stuck in ground, right across garden.'

A.V.W.S.

1951

As One Countryman to Another
THE FORGOTTEN HUNDRED THOUSAND

A BRIGHT PATCH OF flowers or a line of washing among a group of dilapidated huts may sometimes catch the eye of the passer-by, and he may wonder that a wartime camp, hastily erected to serve for the duration, should still be lived in. Most of these former Service camps, however, are situated too far from towns, villages and main roads to attract attention ... Yet there are today twenty-five thousand families, probably not far short of a hundred thousand men, women and children, living in these camps ... It is an indication of the rural housing problem waiting to be tackled that, in the six and a half years since the war ended, the number of occupied huts has not been appreciably diminished, and that local authorities still have lists of people anxious for the chance of such accommodation, for want of better. When a hut becomes completely uninhabitable, it may be demolished, but considerable sums of money are being spent every year, on Ministry instructions, to keep the rest in some sort of repair ...

The camps themselves vary a great deal in their condition and type of occupant. Some were invaded by 'squatters'

who, in desperation, helped themselves and received little sympathy from people already comfortably housed. Others were prepared in advance to provide shelter for families awaiting new houses. A few contained buildings that could be converted into reasonably comfortable dwellings, and it is to the credit of many district councils that they have tried to make huts elsewhere as comfortable as circumstances have allowed. But what can be done, for example, to convert Nissen huts, set down in a hurry on concrete rafts, often in exposed positions, ten or twelve years ago, into dwellings fit for families with young children?

... Most serious of all is the problem of the children. Many thousands are growing up in these rural slums, in damp, unhealthy homes – some hardly deserve the name – without the stabilising influence of a well-founded community. The line of washing or curtains in a window may catch the eye of a passer-by, but he can little realise the nature of the conditions in which these unfortunate camp-dwellers must serve their time.

NOR WITCHCRAFT NEETHER

FOR SEVEN YEARS, until he retired, I was fortunate to have Geordie as my cattleman. He was slow, perhaps, but amazingly sure and thorough. In one thing in particular he was never wrong: he could tell within a matter of minutes when a cow or heifer would calve. One night we were in the byre, waiting on a calf to be born. Judging from the behaviour of the cow that we would not have long to wait, I removed my jacket; but Geordie began to fill his pipe, always a deliberate process, and settled himself on a stool. 'Have your smoke,' he said. 'I'll tell ye in good time.' Once again he was right. Within a few minutes of his telling me that we might now expect the calf, it was born – a full hour after I had looked for it.

'Geordie,' I said, as we busied ourselves about the byre, 'how do you know so exactly when a calf is going to be born? I've watched you and the cow for the past hour; you've done nothing, but you're right again. It's magic.' ''Deed it's no magic nor witchcraft neether', he replied with one of his rare smiles. 'I did something and ye saw me do it.' All I had seen him do was to remove a few tangles from the tuft of hair at the end of the cow's tail, and I told him so. 'Ay, I did that,' he said slowly. 'But that wasna all; I had a feel at her bones too, those wee fine bones at the verra tip o' her tail. Afore a coo can let doon her calf she must be fully relaxed, ye ken that. Then, when ye find the wee bones at the tip o' her tail gone soople, when ye can bend them ower as ye might bend your little finger, she's just on the drop. No laddie, it's no magic nor witchcraft neether.'

Norman I. McDiarmid, Stirlingshire

Poaching with Crabs

BY P. FFORDE, HAMPSHIRE

I have this from a man of seventy-five, who started work on market gardens and farms round Southampton when he was six, and was driving a wagon of produce to market at two o'clock in the morning before he was ten: 'The keepers them days was very lively and it didn't do for 'em to catch you out with no nets nor no ferrets. Nets you can drop quick when they comes at you and not show, but it's not so easy getting rid of a ferret, specially when them keepers 'ad a dog as well as a gun. But the fishing folk around the Solent, they didn't need no ferrets to bolt their rabbits for 'em, see? They was a rough lot them days down that way. Fish six months and work on the farms six months. It's an old saying, fruit kills fish, for you can't sell fish no sense once there's fruit about.

Well these men say they got to know a good bury when they was working on the farms. Next time they was down on the shore they'd collect up one or two of them big old king crabs, that's what they'd do. King crabs it 'ad to be, and make a 'arness for them they would, that'd 'old one of them little candlesticks like you might 'ave on a birthday-cake. Take a candle that'd last ten or say fifteen minutes.

'Then they'd wait till a good dark night, when the keepers'd think a poacher couldn't see to work, and not windy weather neither mind, and along they'd go to that there bury they'd marked, and fix that 'arness on that big old king crab, and a long bit of string tied to him, and stand him out of the wind down the bury. Then they'd light that little candle on his back and give him a push and that big old king crab'd go sideways down that bury, slow an' steady. Very steady sideways 'e'd go down that bury, into the dark, with the candle lighted on 'is back, and when the rabbits down that bury woke and saw that big old king crab coming down at 'em with that flaming candle on his back – bolt! You'd ought to see 'em bolt! Ten in one net I've counted myself. Then all the man had to do was collect up all them rabbits and pull back that old king crab and take off his harness and get along back home quick.

'There's ignorant people don't believe that when I tell 'em. But it's true as I stand here and I've seen it with these two eyes.'

1952

COUNTRYMAN CLUB

PRIMROSES UPSIDE DOWN

More than sixty years ago I used to go with my mother to dig up roots of primroses. We planted them upside down, placed a 'cow-pat' over each and covered them with soil; the next year the blooms were pink. My children did it and my grandchildren are doing it now. Often on a Devon hillside, where primroses grew thickly, we found plants with flowers ranging from pale pink to rose-red. I always imagined that cattle or sheep scrambling up the steep slope had scuffed out a root, and the next animal had trodden it in upside down.

V. Grey, Berkshire

A COCK'S STRIDE

When I happened to remark to an old man in the village that the nights were beginning to draw in quickly, he disagreed emphatically, saying that each day got shorter by a fixed amount. This, he asserted, was exactly equal to the stride 'that old cockerel takes across the yard'. He refused to be shaken from this belief, which he had held since he was a boy.

George Cooper, Cumberland

Fellow Feeling

BY TRIPLE BAR

One morning in November I was out on Beaulieu Heath and paused in the lee of one of the tumuli to fill a pipe. After a perfunctory sniff round the dripping gorse bushes, my collie sat down expectantly at my feet … I squatted down to light the pipe, and as I looked over the flickering match, my eye was drawn to two small dots beating up against the wind towards me, twenty or thirty feet above the ground. At a hundred yards I recognised them. The leader was a chaffinch and the bird behind – only just behind – was a hobby.

As I watched, my mind flashed back seven years to that night when I had been bounced by a Jerry fighter and a twenty-minute running fight had followed. I recalled the frantic glances over my shoulder as I tried to see the whereabouts of the attacker, the terrible suspense while, flying straight, I had to wait for him to commit himself to the next attack before I threw in every ounce of my strength to jink the heavy aircraft into violent evasive action. The chaffinch was doing exactly the same. It was waiting for the hobby to pounce and then, in the last split second before the expected impact, twisting on to a new course. After each attack it strove to gain height without giving up too much of its lead.

Automatically I identified myself with the quarry. 'That's right, boy. Keep your height, whatever you do. Watch him, don't turn too early. Wait – wait – now!' I remembered cursing that I could not go faster; that I could not turn quicker. I remembered the sweat running down the side of my nose into my mask, and the strain on my stomach muscles as I forced on full rudder. I wondered vaguely whether birds sweated when they were frightened. The chaffinch was making for its one hope of safety: a thick clump of gorse not twenty yards from where I crouched. It was dead up wind and there were still sixty yards to go.

The hobby had altered its tactics now. The direct stern chase had been getting it nowhere, so it was climbing up after each attack, losing ground the while, then slowly overhauling its prey again at the higher level before making another vertical stoop. Down it came from twenty feet above. 'God!' I thought, 'he hasn't seen him.' But at the last moment the chaffinch jinked violently to the right and was back again on its course to the gorse bush almost before the hobby had gone past. Once more the hobby climbed and the chaffinch drew ahead; once more the gap between them was reduced, and then again that swift dive. When the flurry was over the chaffinch was still there, plugging along a few feet above the ground, and the hobby was climbing away again. Ten yards to go and at least one more attack to dodge.

My pipe dropped to the ground and the dog leapt out of the way when I sprang to my feet, yelling instructions to the chaffinch as, on that other occasion, my gunner had shouted at me: 'He's high astern. He's coming in – now!' The hobby saw the movement and heard the shout. For a fraction of a second it paused before throwing itself into the attack. That pause made just the difference. With a little thud which I heard plainly, the chaffinch flung itself into the gorse bush; one foot and a fiftieth of a second later the hobby, with every feather outspread to avoid disaster, brushed through the topmost spikes and climbed away. A few small feathers, of uncertain origin, hovered for a second or two above the bush before they were swept away on the wind. The hobby hung around for a short while, thirty feet up, then turned and vanished.

I relaxed and looked down at my dog. 'That's one thing we couldn't do, Joe – duck underground. Still, we did at least have a "Lofty" in the tail to answer back.'

1953

Wild Life and Tame

Fox's Guile

Turning a corner, I suddenly came on a fox worrying a hedgehog which was curled in a tight ball. Dog-like, the fox was snuffling and spitting out spines. Then with his paw he pushed the hedgehog over on its back, lifted his leg and shot a steady stream over it. As the hedgehog began to unroll, the fox grabbed it by the belly and trotted off with it in his mouth.

E.G. Barlow, Hertfordshire

A Fruit Grower's Diary

by Raymond Bush

JUNE 2, 1953

Sheltered from rain and arctic winds,
I sat in some comfort beside a fire and
watched the Coronation on television.

JUNE 9, 1953

London a shambles, the parks and stands
still deep in litter and rubbish. 'Bus
traffic at a standstill and gaping crowds
everywhere. I was told that when the rain
poured down on the coloured troops who
lined the route by the Admiralty Arch,
the blanco used on their turbans dissolved
and fell in white rivulets down their faces;
a man was detailed to go up and down
the line wiping them clean.

JUNE 16, 1953

While staying with a friend in Scotland,
a very deaf man of my acquaintance
thought it would be interesting to try
the effect of his electric deaf-aid on the
15-year-old dog. He put it in place,
and when the owner called the dog it
immediately started to its feet, barked
and wagged its tail. It had not heard its
master's voice for years.

> *Sturdy octogenarian, revealing the secret of his rude health: 'Now, I'll tell ye how 'tis. I eats what I like; I drinks what I like. Then I goes to bed an' lets 'em fight it out among theirselves.'*

> *Irish workman, after a heavy shower of sleet in May: "Tis this new time that diz it. Ye see, they pit on the clock an hour ivery day, an' that's goin' on now for years. If ye add all them hours up, ye'll find instead o' May 'tis really only October yit.'*

1954

" *From north Somerset: 'Did 'ee 'ear about Tom Bristow? Cut off the top of 'is vingers, 'e did! Took off two vingers with the zaw. Then ol' Mister Parsons comed along an' Tom zays, "'Ere, Varmer, zee what I done!" An' 'e zays, "'Ow d'ee come to do that then?" Zo Tom zays, "Like this 'ere." An' baggered if 'e didn' cut off top o' t'other un.'* "

Honest Suffolk

L ast summer a girl from the next farm appeared at 6 a.m. at our door. She had been sent to inquire whether we had lost a cow, as one too many had turned up for the morning milking. When we fetched our herd Phyllis was indeed missing and we informed our neighbour of the fact, hatching over the telephone a complicated plot to secure her return. Next day the butcher brought with our meat an envelope from this neighbour. It contained the sum of 8s 4½d for milk removed from Phyllis at the previous morning's milking.

W.T.G. Boul, Suffolk

COUNTRYMAN CLUB

USE FOR SLOW-WORMS

An islander who was forking couch from my field called to me: 'This is good ground, sir; it even grows grass-snakes.' There are no snakes in Guernsey and his discovery proved to be a slow-worm about 9 in. long. I explained what it was and he said: 'When I was working in a granite quarry we often found them among the loose stuff. We used to put them inside our shirts; they'd keep you cool for a whole day.' *W.C.F. Caldwell, Guernsey*

As It Seems to Some of Us

A TIMELY MEASURE

MYXOMATOSIS IS AN ugly word for a virus disease whose effects – tumours, purulent conjunctivitis and severe swelling of the face and hind parts – are uglier still. In Australia, where it was first employed, many millions of rabbits succumbed in a matter of months. In France half the departments were infected in little more than a year after the release of two inoculated animals, and the disease has spread from there to Belgium, Holland and Germany; in some districts of France nine-tenths of the rabbits are said to have been killed. Myxomatosis has been introduced several times into Britain and died out, but the present strain seems to be exceptionally virulent. Since its appearance in Kent and Sussex in October it has crossed the Thames to Essex and Suffolk; by the autumn there may be few counties free from it. While no-one with a spark of humanity would knowingly have introduced it, this need not prevent us from taking advantage of its ravages to press home the attack on the rabbit, an admitted pest, by more humane methods.

A Fruit Grower's Diary
by Raymond Bush

APR. 11, 1954

I read that a Russian scientist is credited with the successful crossing of the bed-bug with the glow-worm. Soon they will be able to see to read in bed. Had he crossed glow-worms and fire-flies, whole streets might have been lit. Our Jamaican nights are brilliant with fire-flies.

AUG. 14, 1954

I read that 70 fried-shellfish shops in Tokio have combined to raise £700 for a shrine for the souls of the shrimps they have sold. I wonder if some of our fried-fish vendors would care to commemorate the dogfish.

A Farmer's Ruminations

BY CLYDE HIGGS

… Seeing the Archers in their thousandth programme did not destroy the pleasant illusion which this fantastic series has built up. At a Birmingham meeting called to discuss farm broadcasting Henry Burtt, a Lincolnshire farmer well known for his interest in seed production, said that farm programmes as a whole were dull and uninspiring; they needed the Dick Barton touch. The Agricultural Advisory Committee of the B.B.C. heard the first recordings, on a close circuit, with some surprise. My early comment was that the extracts from the attractive signature tune at the beginning and end of each episode were too far apart. Later I listened to criticise. Now I am a confirmed Archerite, certainly not to gain farming tips, which are said to occupy 15 per cent of the programme, but to have quarter of an hour's simple and unsophisticated entertainment with the other 10 m. fans.

… Dolly the gander, relict of Walter the goose, was very lonely for three years. This spring we bought him six goslings which he guarded fiercely and reared with a mother's care. I never imagined that a young brood would bring so much happiness to an old gander, nor that he would make such a splendid goose. He may live to a ripe old age like a goose I met recently in Wiltshire. She is guaranteed 46 years old, and when the cows had their cake changed she altered her diet also and laid five eggs. A relation of hers died at the age of 60.

… George is a mechanised bird-scarer. As cherry-picking time approaches, he is on duty from 6 a.m. to 7 p.m., Sundays included. He sits in the middle of an orchard in a rough hut from which lengths of binder twine go out in various directions. To each is attached a short piece of chain resting on a sheet of corrugated iron propped vertically against a tree. At the sight of birds George pulls the appropriate string and rattles the chains like mad. When I inquired if the method was successful, he replied that it was his own invention and had worked for 30 years. The job has its compensations: it is restful and brings in £20 a week.

A Fruit Grower's Diary

by Raymond Bush

MAR. 23, 1955

Asked to collect caviar for a cocktail party. I was offered some at 6s 6d and some at 27s 6d a tin. I am told that the cheap variety is the spawn of a toad cultivated in Australia.

JULY 14, 1955

Some of the tallest and largest cumulus clouds I have ever seen piled up overhead and moved south-west. Ascot had the brunt of it with 40 people struck by lightning.

JULY 17, 1955

Today, the hottest this summer, a shaded thermometer in a sheltered garden in Hampshire registered 96°F.

JULY 18, 1955

The heat wave collapsed with a 30° drop in the temperature, and something was bound to happen after that. In north Hampshire we had no more than drizzle, but in south Dorset 7.2 in. of rain fell in 24 hours and Weymouth was badly flooded. In 1952 Longstone Barrow (1,500 ft high) in north Devon had 9 in. on August 15. That and more than 7 in. near by resulted in the Lynmouth disaster. Bruton in Somerset holds the English record for rainfall with 9.56 in. on June 28, 1917.

Why Skin a Rabbit?

When I was living in the Windward Islands I bought a rabbit – there considered a delicacy – and sat skinning it on the veranda steps. I had freed the hind legs and was peeling the skin off the back when a group of smallholders stopped to watch me. 'Why does he do that?' one asked another. 'Don't know,' was the reply. The French patois was difficult to follow and I could catch only a phrase here and there. I cut round the ears to free the head, for I am part Scot and that sensible race knows how tasty is the brain, once the knack of splitting down the skull has been mastered. As an old dame passed she took one look at the skin and fur hanging free, spat and said: *'Sacré nom! C'est comme cochon.'* This was too much for me. 'What interests you?' I asked a lad who had joined the group. 'We have never seen the skin of a rabbit,' he said. 'We dip our rabbits in boiling water and pull out the hairs. It takes a long time and is most tedious.' I left the group passing the pelt from hand to hand, discussing the phenomenon with much gesticulation

J.A.N. Burra

Guinea-Pigs and Rats

He met me at the gate of the compound as I was returning home. He was not one of my own men, but I knew him as a local villager. 'Well, what do you want?' I asked. 'An advance of ten rupees, sahib.' He was very persistent. 'Sahib, I must have the money. The moneylender is going to seize my cow.' Moneylenders were my pet aversion, a fact generally known in the locality, so this was his trump card. I still would not play, however, and finally he asked me to buy a pair of guinea-pigs. Thus I became the owner of two of these animals, at much over the market price I felt sure.

They were placed in a small cage outside the kitchen and the cook fed them. I saw them occasionally, but otherwise took little interest in them. Shortly afterwards I went on long leave, so a syce took charge of them. A month or so after my return he asked me if I wanted the guinea-pigs back, and I told him that he might keep them if they were of any use to him. They were, he assured me. Since he had taken them into his house he had seen no rats, though previously they had been a great nuisance.

Years later, in another part of India,

the manager of an estate complained of rats in his bungalow 'Keep guinea pigs,' I told him. It was a joke and the subject of much merriment when we dined with the doctor that night, so I let the subject drop. But a week or so afterwards, going round a neighbouring estate, I spotted a box with three guinea-pigs outside the kitchen of an assistant's bungalow.

I said nothing until the evening at the club where I twitted the young man, who was new to the district, about them. 'What's the idea of keeping guinea-pigs outside your kitchen?' I asked him. 'To keep the rats away, of course,' came the reply. Apparently in his previous district most planters had kept them for that purpose.

R. Jeff

Bulorns, Kenacks and Lizamoo

My Cornish ex-sailor gardener is 'some old ting tavao', but between intervals of chatter he does useful work on my splat of ground. He takes a braave spur (good while) to get through, but he can always find time to smell the gillyflowers and to notice the thrush at its anvil breaking snail-shells, or as he puts it, 'the grey-bird scattin' the bulorns' – sometimes he calls them jan-jakes – 'to sherds'. He digs a straight vore for the beans, pausing to throw a bully (pebble) at the cat because she chased away a pedn-paly (blue tit). With his garden fork, which he calls an evil, he lifts a burn of dried grasses for the mabyers' (pullets') nests, and he gives them a few kenacks (worms). Mizzle or skewy (showery) rain is good for sticking plant, by which he means planting

out all types of cabbage and broccoli and stanking or treading them firm in the ground. The soft weather brings on the weeds – drill-draw, keggas and lizamoo, known to me as small bindweed, hemlock and cow-parsnip. Weeding he finds 'a sparey (tedious) ole job' and cutting the skedge (privet) not much better. The rain always seems to come when he has a few tubbins (turfs) to burn: these and the damp cricks (twigs) in the bonfire make some smeech. His griglan or heather broom is handy for sweeping paths or to place in the arm of the bucca, whose realistic hand-painted face frightens more than the crows. A day too wet to work in the garden is 'a day gone in to the King'.

Gladys Hunkin, Cornwall

1956

Blobbing for Eels

BY JOAN FORMAN

The old fenmen who caught eels on the grand scale used hives or nets such as are still employed in many parts of the country. Ordinary coarse tackle is also sometimes used. But perhaps the most exciting method, though far and away the most messy, is 'blobbing' or 'babbing', as it is called in some districts. My father first introduced me to it when I was still too young to argue, so I took his word for it that it was the best method.

The 'blob' is intricate in appearance but simple enough to make. As the youngest member of the party I was given the task of cutting scores of yards of plain knitting worsted, which forms the basis of the tackle, into lengths varying from four to six feet. But when it came to baiting them I went on strike: a choice of lobworms or raw chicken-gut for stringing on to the yards of worsted did not appeal to me. The men of the party threaded the bait with large darning needles, pushing each piece to the centre of a length of wool. They then tied the ends of the wool together and divided the whole length of baited line into four or more loops which they secured, like a lover's knot, round the middle. We now had a succession of baited blobs, each with four or five loops.

'I screamed and yelled'

Illustration from a vivid article about gypsies, by Dominic Reeve. At the age of four, he had his ears pierced by his grandmother for the traditional boys' ear-rings.

If the water is not static the blobs must be weighted to prevent their floating to the surface. Any 2- to 3-oz metal weight will serve, except in fast-running water. We attached ours about an inch and a half below the centre of each blob. Finally the blob was secured by a length of cord to a stout stick which would serve as a lever to lift the catch over the side of the boat. Since there was no hook for the eels to bite, they would be held only by their teeth entangled in the worsted; and the slightest knock of line or blob against the side of the boat would be enough to lose the catch.

Danny's Pet

by Armorel Garrett

At the head of Loch Torridon, rounding the bend of the road which leads to the village of Annat, I came on a straggling herd of cows indolently swinging their way to the milking byre on the green. The advance party had almost reached the first cottage, but three or four dawdlers were delayed by the attractions of a weedy bank and some were even straying among the rocks round the path to Strathcarron. Between those elderly beasts grown obedient to the sense of organisation and the more rebellious ones still anxious to assert their freedom a small black-faced ewe was galloping up and down. Her fleece reached almost to the ground, like the armour of a medieval war-horse, and flounced all in one piece as she ran about her self-appointed task of restoring the unity of the herd. As I watched her tiny black hooves under this mountain of wool, Sir John Suckling's lines came to mind: 'Her feet beneath her petticoat, Like little mice, stole in and out'. She paused for a moment to talk with me in the intervals of calling to the laggard cows but was soon off again at a gallop to join those which had already rounded the last bend for home.

I stopped to discuss the ewe's strange behaviour with Mr. McDonald who lived near by. 'That's Danny's Pet,' he said. 'He brought her up on the bottle and she lives with his cows. She won't have anything to do with sheep. She sleeps on the green outside the byre, and every morning when the cows are turned out she shepherds them up the glen. Sometimes they go many miles, but every evening at sundown she brings them home again. The cows seem to recognise her as the boss.'

Outwitting the Ostrich

BY RUTH EADEN

One hot afternoon in January I was driving home across the Naro Moru plains of Kenya with my Kikuyu garden boy. Standing six feet in his socks and strong as an ox, Wanyuki has a love and understanding of animals which in an African is remarkable. He was on the look-out for game, and when he shouted, 'Look! *Buni!*' I stopped the car. Among some distant mimosa thorn trees he had seen eight hen ostriches, rather drab-looking in their grey-brown plumage, and a magnificent cock with white plumes creaming from shining black pinions, head raised in arrogant inquiry. The surrounding wild oat-grass was alive with their chicks, hardly taller than the grass itself. Wanyuki counted more than a hundred, which was probably near the mark, allowing for mishaps in hatching and after, for the ostrich lays a clutch of up to twenty eggs.

We left the car noiselessly to get a closer view and Wanyuki, who was wearing a white shirt, possessed himself of the old bath-towel that does duty as a car duster, winding it turban fashion round his head. He then advanced towards the ostriches with arms crooked and flapping like wings and began to dance, whereupon the cock lowered its head and rushed to give battle. There is something obscene about a running ostrich, with the pounding hackney action of its great bare pink legs, its plumage bouncing like a ballet skirt in third-rate opera. In my car I paced one over half a mile at thirty-six miles per hour.

The oncoming cock was now at top speed, and I called to Wanyuki to come back; he would stand no chance against its downward sledge-hammer kick. But he continued to dance and shouted over his shoulder: 'I'm all right. I know all about *buni*. I'm not afraid.' Not till the ostrich was within thirty yards of him did he stop dancing, snatch the towel from his head and flap it at the bird. Greatly to my relief the creature swerved, braked hard, and came to a dead stop. It then lay flat on its side and remained motionless. 'Look now,' cried the jubilant Wanyuki, 'he pretends to be dead. He wants me to go close up to him, when he would jump up and kill me with his foot.'

There was a pause while the boy once more donned the towel and began to dance. Instantly the ostrich scrambled to its feet and charged again. 'See now,' Wanyuki exclaimed in tones of ecstasy, 'this *buni* is very, very angry; his head has turned red.' And when the bird had come still closer the towel-waving performance was repeated.

Meanwhile three young cocks had appeared on the scene and were taking advantage of their opportunity to make advances to the eight hens. As the prostrate cock rose for a second time it caught sight of the fast-working intruders. Instantly it abandoned Wanyuki and tore off to deal with the fresh threat to its harem. The young cocks fled for their lives but not before one, less quick off the mark than the others, was speeded on its way by a kick well directed to the tail.

Wanyuki, a dazzle of white teeth marking the grin that spread from ear to ear, was triumphant: 'Now, *memsaabu*, you see I do know all about *shauri ya buni*' – the affairs of the ostrich.

In the Country and Out of It

I HAD A cheery visit from John Walker, editor of a periodical of character, the *Essex Farmers' Journal* ... About 1936 [he] was one of a party of journalists who saw Harry Ferguson demonstrate the first of his tractors. 'He called it the "iron horse" and said that it would eventually displace nearly every horse in the country and be the means of greatly increasing food production throughout the world. I think we all thought he was a rather mad Irishman.'   *J.W.R.S.*

COUNTRYMAN CLUB

VIOLET LEAVES AND CANCER

A friend of our family, the elderly wife of a doctor, who was told that her internal cancer could not be operated on, saw an article in a medical paper in which two doctors recorded a cancer cure by the use of violet leaves. We then lived in Radnorshire, and she came and gathered violet leaves from our garden, made tea of them while they were still fresh (this would seem to be essential) and drank it at intervals during the day. In a fairly short time she reported that the haemorrhage had stopped. Then the pain went and she began to look much better. She was still well when, some years later, we lost touch with her. In the same district a 'wise woman' was also reputed to have cured cancer in this way, but I cannot myself vouch for her.   *Marjorie Tolson, Yorks*

Tails

WHILE OUR EXPERIENCE as vets in many ways runs parallel with that of our medical friends, in the matter of tails we have the field to ourselves. Nearly all our patients have one, useful or merely ornamental, and our attention is often drawn to it. I hope the once vexed question of docking horses is now settled, but a good many puppies are still deprived of their tails by breeders or, shamefacedly, by us. The only excuse for the operation, barring disease of the tail, is fashion. Some breeds are unlikely to do well at shows unless they are thus mutilated. The only excuse that I can make myself is that, if I refuse, someone unskilled may do it, and for the puppy's sake it may as well be done properly.

In the first few days of life the pain and inconvenience are momentary and no worse than is caused by removal of the dew-claws, which is more justifiably done at the same time. The story is very different with a puppy eight or nine weeks old – often of mixed parentage – whose career is in no way likely to be blighted by possession of a tail, but whose new owner, or his wife or neighbour, thinks it ought to be removed. A minor operation is needed, with tourniquet, local anaesthetic, stitches and bandage. Fortunately a direct refusal to operate is seldom called for. Most people can be talked out of it, like the lady who brought me her two-month-old mongrel because her neighbour wanted to bite off its tail. She had been told that worms, fits and possibly rabies were the probable results of neglect, and that at least the puppy would never thrive; all its strength would go to its tail.

It is a common idea that a cat's vital principle lives in its tail. Many otherwise healthy cats with injured tails have been brought to me for destruction, their injuries being assumed to be automatically fatal. The average cat is remarkably careless with its tail. My own half-bred Siamese frequently puts hers in the fire while parading on the hearth and, unless rescued, does not remove herself until it bursts into flames. Then she moves away with dignity in a cloud of singed fur, muttering a curse at the bystander, who is assumed to be responsible. I have treated many cats which have lost their tails to trains – one lost half of his by this means, and the other half went the same way before the stump was healed – laundry machinery, falling crates or closing doors. They do not seem to suffer any disability.

… It seems a pity that we have a monopoly of this appendage. It can only be lack of material that deprives many a potentially brilliant caudologist of his rightful place in Harley Street.

By a Veterinary Surgeon

"Lincolnshire countryman's comment on neighbour with large feet: "E'd 'a bin a tall 'un if 'e 'adn't 'ad ower much turned up at the bottom.' "

Second to None

by Wendy Wood

In races and steeplechases how often does a horse that has shed its rider romp home in style! But at the Cape I many times witnessed a race in which there were no riders. A firm had two breweries, one on the slopes of Table Mountain and the other two miles away, on the flat. When the top brewery was no longer required it was converted into stables. All the firm's teams, six mules to a wagon, amounting to some hundred and fifty animals, were outspanned in a big yard at the lower brewery. As both man and beast were anxious for a meal, the release was achieved in quick time. Once all the harness was off, the big gates were opened and the mules stampeded for the stables.

Everyone in the district knew to the minute when the cavalcade was due, which was just as well, for the mules charged down Station Road at full gallop, crossed the main street with its tram lines, pelted madly up a road ironically called Sans Souci and over a wooden bridge where their hooves made thunder, and rushed up a steep hill leading to a narrow path by a river. There was a high wall on one side of this path and on the other a steep bank, down which a mule would sometimes be shoved. It would then arrive in the river and scream with fury as it tried to regain its place. But the greatest hazard was still ahead: a narrow gate which let only one mule through the twelve-foot wall at a time, so that a man on the other side could count them. Quite often two, with the head of a third, would be jammed squealing in the orifice, while the rest piled up one on top of another till some could almost have got over the wall.

When they had won through they celebrated with a wild flinging of heels and hee-hees of joy, but their troubles were not over. An old Scots Greys N.C.O. was in charge of the stables and would not have them dirtied. So in the yard commanded by the wicket gate there were large dumps of straw, and to one or other of these each mule had to pay its contribution before being allowed into the building. The faces of some thus hindered were comical. Soon, however, all were contentedly munching oats in stables with bedding plaited at the edges like the mane of a show Clydesdale; often a week went by without the need to disturb it. Over the door of those immaculate stables was displayed the regimental motto, 'Second to None'.

1958-1967

'Probable result of the poultry mania.'

Prosperity and Optimism

D uring the 1960s in particular, there began to be a much greater awareness of subjects such as ecology, conservation, pollution and animal welfare (including concerns about 'factory farming'). Early in the decade there were signs of environmental problems; and major crises towards the end of this period (e.g. the Aberfan disaster and the 'Torrey Canyon' oil spillage) prompted demands for action – often, it would seem, from those who did not actually live and work in the countryside but used it for recreational purposes. The number of countryside visitors was growing fast and the number of cars on the roads in 1966 had doubled to 7 million in ten years. In the early 1960s rural areas were being particularly hard hit by the ruthless closure of railway branch lines under Dr.Beeching's axe.

Many new farm buildings were springing up all over the country, and mechanisation was at full blast. Britain entered the Common Market, which brought its own hopes and difficulties. Science was moving into farming in a big way, and it was noticeable that research into agriculture was based on science rather than on experience in the field. There is a feeling through the pages of

(Above) Old Punch *cartoon (January 1853) reproduced in Leonora Hering's 1967 article about breeding fancy poultry for the shows.*

The Countryman that the old arts of husbandry, both of livestock and of crops, were being overridden by the use of 'science' to increase productivity, and this was alarming to many people. The seminal book by Rachel Carson, *Silent Spring*, was published in 1962 – a real wake-up call that still resounds today.

There was also growing pressure on country villages as people moved out of the towns seeking a better way of life, but not necessarily contributing to the rural society in which they had opted to live.

In the autumn of 1961 the familiar dark green paper cover was changed to a heavier, textured one in a glossier leaf green, with line drawings on a white background, and the price rocketed instantly to five shillings. It would jump again, to six shillings, in the spring of 1967.

John Cripps wrote many pages for an obituary of J W Robertson Scott in the Spring 1963 issue and included this illustration of the Founder Editor's home, Idbury Manor, as seen from its gardens; the house was the editorial office for the journal throughout R.S.'s editorship.

The irrepressible Clyde Higgs died very suddenly in 1963. A newcomer to the journal's pages in 1966 was farmer Tristram Beresford, whose every article was stimulating, deeply thoughtful and knowledgeable; he continued to contribute regularly for a decade, until he moved to farm in France.

Over the Christmas of 1962 J.W. Robertson Scott died. He had been born in Wigton, Cumberland, in 1866 – in a very different era. The changes he had seen in the countryside in his own lifetime were huge. The 'Swinging Sixties' and all they embraced were alien to him.

1958

An article by D. Valentine (Summer 1958) described a wonderful range of haystacks seen on India's Deccan plateau and around the perimeter of the Great Indian Desert.

A New Defence Against Rats

BY H.A. LINDSAY

In Adelaide, Harry and Nigel Oliphant, brothers of the nuclear physicist Professor Marcus Oliphant, have designed an improved form of ultra-violet lamp which, by sterilising the air in hospital wards, reduces the chance of cross-infection among patients, particularly infants. This same lamp, installed in a butcher's cool room, was found to kill spores of mould and bacteria, reducing meat wastage during a weekend of hot weather from as much as ten per cent to almost nil. A similar saving was effected in premises where fresh fruit was stored.

One day a man walked into the Oliphants' laboratory and said: 'There is some kind of black magic about those little lamps of yours. We haven't had a rat or mouse in our chocolate factory since they were installed.' Investigation showed that, in any premises where the lamps were kept switched on day and night, there was never a sign of rat, mouse, cockroach or lazy moth. Cheese, biscuits, nuts, raisins, ham and similar foodstuffs, which are usually attacked by the pests at every opportunity, could be left uncovered. A fruit merchant installed some of the lamps in his store, and weeks went by without any sign of rats or mice on the premises. Thinking that these pests had now learnt to avoid them, he switched off the lamps to save current. When he opened the doors next morning a scene of devastation met his gaze. Hordes of rats had entered during the night and played havoc. He had saved electricity to the value of about eighteen pence but had to send £80 worth of fruit to the rubbish dump …

> " *One evening in May my wife and I found the children's roundabouts in Fitz Park, Keswick, deserted but not for long. Sheep which had been grazing walked to one of them, and the leader jumped on the platform, setting it in motion. As others quickly followed, its speed increased; and the whole flock had a ride, jumping on and off, some more than once. We were told that this had happened many times when no children were about.* " R.W. Barnes

A Farmer's Ruminations

BY CLYDE HIGGS

The horrible possibilities of artificial insemination were brought home to me when I looked at semen in deep-freeze chests in which 28,000 doses were stored, at −70°F., in a sinister mass of fiendishly bubbling dry ice. Some of it was five years old and as virile as on the day it was collected. Experimental consignments sent oversea have given a conception rate higher than that obtained at home. For animal breeding artificial insemination has come to stay. The implications of its use are just too fantastic. Progeny testing long after the bull is dead may decide if his strain is to be used. A very few bulls would influence the trend of breeding.

A new centre was opened recently by the Hampshire Cattle Breeders' Society, which was founded in 1944 on borrowed money. This has all been repaid, and sufficient reserves accumulated to justify an expenditure of £85,000 on the new centre. A cooperative enterprise with a membership of more than 4,000, it is dealing with 60 per cent of the cattle population in the area. The gigantic bull-barn, 260ft long, houses 29 bulls of seven breeds. They are exercised on an electrically driven 'treadmill' which leads them round by chains attached to their rings. In spite of the mechanical monotony they looked extremely well. Work is being done on pigs – a more difficult job, with a conception rate of 43 per cent against 67 per cent for cattle.

A county librarian vouches for the following tale. A small boy asked for and was given a book on rabbits, but he returned it next day: 'Nae use.' A second book quickly came back too: 'That's nae use either. Hae ye onythin' else aboot rabbits?' When the boy returned a third book with the same comment, the assistant asked him what he wanted to know about rabbits. 'Breedin',' answered the boy. 'Oh, but goodness me,' expostulated the assistant, 'I'm sure there is something in all three books about breeding.' 'Och aye,' finished off the boy, 'but they're a' for fowk wi' twa rabbits.' Alistair Steven

1959

Sex Problem in Devon

When my aunt used to say, 'Everything in Devon is "he" except a tom-cat,' I thought it was just her little joke; but later I went to live in the south-east of the county and found it was quite true. One evening I asked a farmer how many cows he had, and he said: 'I got twenny-two bullicks' ('u' as in 'dull'). 'And how many milking cows?' I asked; to which he replied 'Them's bullicks.' Often at night we would be roused by the cry: 'Dan, the goat's loose; he's in the garden,' and the sleepy reply: 'Right on, I'll deal with him.' Yet this goat became the mother of twins. Our sixteen-year-old maid said of the dog they had at home: 'Name's Nellie, same's me.' I asked her how they knew who was wanted when someone called the name, and she answered: 'Us says "Come on daag" an''e comes runnin'; lil gurl daag 'e is.' She also told me of a 'lil pheasanty hen, ever s'funny lil to-ad, with 'is tail all t'wunside; but you wait till 'e lays 'is eggs.' Yet in question form the sex is reversed, as: 'Uncle's gone 'Oniton market.''Is 'er?' Or: 'I seen your brother up aw-ver.' 'Ah? Whur's 'er tu?' And sure enough, in accordance with my aunt's dictum, the white tom who used to visit our black cat was always spoken of as 'she', in spite of frequent piebald proof to the contrary.   *R.C.*

A variety of 'owl holes' in barns around Wharfedale, illustrated in a letter from reader Ursula W. Brighouse (Devon) in the autumn of 1959. Most barn builders deliberately created entrances for barn owls – nature's rat-catchers.

1960

Incidents of Bird Life

SPARROW ON BACK

The cock sparrow was caught when he flew into a garage, and held on his back in a little girl's hand. As she rotated her finger only an inch or so from his head, he followed it with his beak. She kept her finger just above the beak and the bird lay quiet, allowing her to transfer him to the tabletop. Then, moving the finger slowly up and down, she gradually increased the distance between it and the beak. The sparrow watched intently and, when the finger was about 3in. from him, made a lightning dart away. He was recaught several times and behaved similarly on each occasion. – *Walter Jarchow, W. Germany* [As bird ringers know, many small birds react like this when held on the back, even without the 'hypnotic' effect of the finger, though I have quietened sparrows in the manner here described. Among garden birds chaffinches and robins also make good 'subjects', but I have not succeeded in hypnotising tits, which in the normal course of their active lives often hang upside down, whereas most birds never do so. I know of no proper study of the condition. – *B.C.*]

COUNTRYMAN CLUB

MADONNA LILY CURE

My grandmother, who came from Exeter, used to preserve Madonna lily petals in brandy, and a wonderful cure they made. – *E. Stevenson, Worcs.* * No other dressing was used in my Sussex home and the results were always good. – *J. Child, Cornwall.* * My grandmother, who lived in Offton, Suffolk, kept our mother supplied with Madonna lily petals steeped in brandy for our childhood cuts, and the cure never failed. – *E.M. Watkinson, Essex*

BELIEVE IT OR NOT

On a visit to friends at Hove I noticed a 2-in. band chalked round each gate-post, about 10 in. from it. An inquiry elicited the facts that the dogs of the neighbourhood used to call there, and that when the daily help commented on this to the milkman, who happened to be an old countryman, he had advised her to get some chalk and draw the bands. During the ten days of my visit they served their purpose …
– *W.J. Dore-Dennis, Surrey*

Barwick's Follies

Travellers on the road to Dorchester, south of Yeovil, are often puzzled by [some] oddly shaped towers. They serve as reminders that ours has not been the only age in which relief work has had to be found for the unemployed. About 1830 Yeovil's famous glove trade, in common with many other industries, was feeling the effects of depression; workhouses were multiplying, and in some districts there were disorders. To provide employment a local squire, Messiter by name, had four towers built. These sham antiques were almost certainly intended to beautify the landscape, and perhaps also to mark the confines of Barwick Park.

The tower carried by a broad archway supports a figure which may be Hermes, messenger of the gods. It is said locally to commemorate Jack, who used to run to and from London with messages for the Messiters. He trained on treacle and is said to come down from the pinnacle at midnight to quench his treacle-induced thirst at the lake. Jack the Treacle Eater is the name by which the statue is known, and legend has it that if treacle is placed under the folly at night it will be gone by morning. There is another story that a poacher killed a policeman and hid for seven months in the tower, where his wife brought him food.

The tower resembling an old-fashioned factory chimney, about fifty feet high, is known as the Fish Tower, after a fish weathervane which used to surmount the iron cage of a well-head that caps the column. The Needle, a thin column of random rubble overlooking the main road to Dorchester and now almost hidden by trees and undergrowth, is tilted drunkenly at the top. The remaining tower, with three arches at the base, is commonly regarded as one of the finest follies in Britain. It, too, is built of rough stone, except for the smooth apex with a stone ball at the top. All the way up the sides are rings of small square holes which light the interior of the seventy-foot cone.

Reece Winstone

> *A Westmorland farm worker found with his 'drinking' [elevenses] a huge slice of jam pasty which obviously had little inside it. 'I'm thinkin' as 'ow this is a bit o' I'm-'ere-where's-thou-possty,' he remarked. Asked to explain, he said: 'This 'ere's corrant jam possty, but there's nobbut two corrants in't an' they gets lonesome and shouts to each other, 'I'm 'ere, where's thou?'*

Cat Logic

BY PHYLLIS LYTH

You are a human and I am a cat
But I don't go throwin' things, cursin' and kickin'
Whenever I see you eat pieces of chicken—
I say, 'Well, it's nature,' and leave it at that.

If I were a human and you were a cat
I wouldn't go wringin' my hands and sob-sobbin'
If one day for dinner you fancied a robin—
I'd say, 'We're alike then,' and leave it at that.

COUNTRYMAN CLUB

CAT'S EYES

One wintry afternoon I was walking with a friend in south Devon, and a cottager at Mothecombe was directing us to Holbeton, where we hoped to get tea. If the tide was out, she said, it would take about an hour along the beach; but if the tide was in, it would take much longer by road. Rather to our surprise, as the cottage was some distance from the shore, her little boy volunteered to find out the state of the tide. He did not go towards the beach but indoors, and returned almost immediately to tell us that the tide was in. When we asked him how he knew, he said he could tell by the cat's eyes. He was in no doubt about it and turned out to be right, so we gave up the idea of tea and went home. Some years later at St. Malo, on the opposite side of the Channel, I read in an article that, before the building of the causeway that joins Mont St. Michel with the mainland, Breton country people living some distance from the shore always looked at the cat's eyes to see whether the tide would allow them to cross to the Mount.　　　　*C.H.D. Grimes, Devon*

A USE FOR COW-DUNG

In Kenya we were driving in fencing posts during the hot season, when the ground was rock-hard. My Kikuyu head-man collected fresh cow-dung and plastered it over the sites for each post, which was then driven in without difficulty.

Lt-Col. T.B. Butt, Co. Kildare

Wild Life and Tame

FROGS' SCREAMS

The request last quarter for eye-witness accounts of frogs screaming while being devoured by grass-snakes brought us many letters.

Among the creatures which have been seen to cause frogs to scream are grass-snakes, an adder and slow-worm, several hens and as many cats, a shrew, rat, mole and crow, and a number of human beings equipped with sticks. In all these incidents the behaviour of the frogs was broadly the same, although the cries struck witnesses variously as a thin high-pitched whistle, a peculiar plaintive cry and a mellow breathy scream. Always they have made a strong impression on the hearer, whether he was reminded of the scream of a young child or a rabbit's squeal; and several correspondents have expressed amazement that so small a creature could make so great a noise. One lady and her neighbour were both awakened by screams in the garden at night; on going out to investigate they found a cat playing with a frog.

The screams have usually been not only loud but prolonged. There are reports of 'a loud continuous scream' and 'cries continued without intermission'; on one occasion they continued for a full minute after a frog had been rescued from a Muscovy duck and released in an orchard. This seems to dispose convincingly of the view that the cry is caused simply by the expulsion of air from the lung as the frog is swallowed.

If further evidence is required, there are several instances of frogs screaming before they are attacked; indeed one appears to have held a cat successfully at bay by emitting an ear-piercing noise each time the feline raised its paw. The slow-worm made no attempt to approach nearer to a large frog at the other end of a doorstep, but the more it wriggled the louder were the screams. One correspondent recalls how, as a young boy, he made a frog jump repeatedly until it let out a thin high-pitched scream; and another several times saw an old farm worker wriggle a stick behind not a frog but a toad to 'mak' un cry', which it did. Most remarkable, perhaps, is the incident of a large frog which was seen in a withy bed with its mouth wide open, screaming loudly, and was then grabbed by a mole; this came from under leaves and grass and, after being disturbed, returned within seconds to the attack.

1962

The Open Road

by Victor Meek

One day in 1922 I decided that, as soon as I had served my time in India with the R.A.F., I would buy a donkey, load it with a tent, small trade articles, a blow-lamp, solder and other tinkering equipment and travel Britain foot-loose and fancy-free. I would get a pedlar's licence, to be all right with the Law. My training as a fitter would serve, though I would have to learn a bit more about soldering. Handy and willing, I would find all doors open to me. I worked out the costs. Forty pounds should cover everything: donkey, tent and equipment. So for the next three years I made an allotment home of nine-pence a day.

I came back to England in 1925 and, while on demob leave, called at the local police station. The sergeant was a smart young man, efficient but friendly. He took some particulars of my intentions and then asked, 'Will you be carrying a pack or pushing a tinker's wheel?'

'I'm going to have a donkey,' I told him, feeling a bit self-conscious.

He put down the pencil. 'In that case it's not our cup of tea at all. We issue pedlars' certificates at five bob a go, provided of course our inquiries as to character and so forth are satisfactory. But the Pedlars Act, 1871, deals only with people who travel without horse or other beast bearing or drawing burden, trading on foot, selling goods for immediate delivery or offering for sale skill in handicraft such as tinkering and chair-mending, grinding knives – that sort of thing.'

'What does a donkey make me then, sarge?'

'A hawker, lad. Nothing to do with us. You need a customs and excise licence costing two pounds, and they won't issue one unless you produce a certificate of good character signed by a clergyman and two local residents, or by a justice, or by a local police inspector who knows you. Then you'd need your name on every package of goods you carried, and you'd have to produce the licence on demand.' He gave a chuckle and added, 'But if you trade without one we can't summons you.'

'Why not?'

'Because the Hawkers Act,1888, happens to be an Excise Act, so the police can only arrest you.'

I decided to abandon Neddy. 'What if I travel on foot?'

'Then you just need a pedlar's certificate.'

'And you won't arrest me if I leave it at home, I suppose?'

'Not only may but must, lad. The Vagrancy Act, 1824, lays down a fine of five pounds on the policeman with a soft heart. He must arrest anyone found offending against the Act, and uncertificated pedlars are included.'

I walked to the door. It was not as I had dreamed it would be while in India.

'There's a way round it, lad', he said. I turned back. I was beginning to admire him.

'If you don't sell anything, but just offer for sale your skill in handicraft, you can have your donkey and come under neither Act.'

It was too late. The open road had ceased to beckon. 'No thanks, sergeant,' I said. 'I don't fancy the idea any more, somehow. I'll try something else.'

He would have made a good salesman. 'There's exceptions. You can sell vegetables, fish, fruit, victuals and coal – and books if authorised in writing by the publishers. Then again there's …'

I interrupted him. 'But there's more snags, I'll bet.'

'Well, of course, if you pitch a tent or encamp on the highway, which includes the footway, you're liable to be knocked off under the Highways Act, 1835. And don't forget the viz.'

'The viz?'

'Visible means of subsistence, lad. Most of them keep a tanner in their boot. Then they can sleep out without interference.'

'Vagrancy Act?' I suggested.

'That's right. Section 4. You're getting the idea.'

I made up my mind. 'Can I have one of those leaflets, sarge?' I asked, pointing to the desk.

'Now you're talking, lad,' he said with enthusiasm; 'that's more like a job. All the walking you could wish for.'

I sent in my application to join the police that night, and served my time for a pension.

> "*A farm worker got a job near the coast, and on the afternoon of his arrival it was so foggy that passing ships were sounding their fog-horns. Jerking his thumb sea-wards, he remarked to the farmer: 'It's time them cows were milked.'* "

Cooking by the Sun

BY PHILIP ZEALEY

At the National Physical Laboratory in Delhi I met a United Nations scientist who was helping to organise a scientific translation service. He had taken very seriously the possibility of utilising solar energy. 'It just angered me,' he said, 'to think of all the superfluous sunshine going to waste.' So in his spare time he had helped Indian scientists to construct several types of solar concentrator for experimental purposes. Understandably none would be suitable for domestic use, but he knew that a small cooker with a parabolic reflector had been developed in Africa. It was rather costly and, under working conditions, the metal parabola soon tarnished; so it had not proved very serviceable.

My Delhi acquaintance told me that he was working on an idea for a solar concentrator for domestic cooking; it would cost about 5 rupees (7s 6d). Several months later, on my next visit, I found him in the garden of his bungalow. Water was boiling merrily in a metal jar on a tripod, at the foot of which two wooden frames lay on the ground in line with the sun, each containing a small collection of handbag mirrors so arranged as to concentrate reflected sunlight at the base of the water jar. 'The mirrors cost a few annas each,' he explained, 'and I got a village carpenter to make the frames on my veranda. I think that, in quantity, each cooking unit could be made for five rupees. The other afternoon my cook prepared my supper on this one, and he is quite enthusiastic.'

Dickory Dock

I HAD BEEN TROUBLED with mice in the kitchen; and though I tried all types of trap, keeping a cat and filling up holes as fast as they were made, the mice always came back. One night, disturbed by their scrabblings but still half asleep, I suddenly thought I would get the alarm clock – one of the old-fashioned sort – and put it on the kitchen floor. Its loud tick reverberated through the boards, and in the morning there was no sign of a mouse. The following night I rewound the clock and put it back on the floor, with a second one alongside and some tempting cake; this remained untouched. I now keep both clocks on the floor, ticking merrily, and have not seen another mouse.

A.B. Quine

1963

Nine Lives

BY ISABEL ANSFORD

Orphy was a Black Orpington on our New Zealand farm. She was deserted by her mother before she was properly out of the shell, perhaps because all her relatives were White Leghorns. We shelled the orphan, wrapped her in Father's singlet and unintentionally par-baked her in the oven, a hazard which she survived much better than did the singlet.

Two days later she nose-dived into the drinking-trough and was all but drowned. Having been revived once more in the oven, she proceeded to fall into a tin of soft soap, from which we rescued her with the copper-stick. We chased away her relatives before they could devour her for her fat content; but with wings matted and useless she proved easy prey for a cruising hawk and was carried off on a trans-paddock flight. Hearing our shrieks, Father came out with a gun, and his first shot brought down the hawk, with Orphy still alive though featherless. All five children charged to the rescue, but the cat got there first and bolted under the shed with us in pursuit. We reached Orphy just in time, and if Small Brother got stuck under a beam, who cared?

Not long after this ordeal she sought to vary the monotonous barnyard fare and fell into a preserving pan full of cooling jam. We managed to scrape her clean and hoped that, a sadder and wiser fowl, she would live to a ripe old age. It was not to be, for, having laid a couple of tiny eggs, Orphy grew spurs and a comb, and died in a spectacular battle with a genuine rooster, crowing to her last breath. After all, she had something to crow about.

" Half-way down a steep winding hill near Egton, North Yorkshire, we stopped the car to ask an old woman at her garden gate if the hill was dangerous. 'Not 'ere it isn't;' she told us, 'it's down at bottom where they all kills theirsens.' "

Books about the Country

SILENT SPRING

TWENTY YEARS AGO, I remember, I slipped down to the pub and bought a crate of beer which we drank round the threshing drum to celebrate our first field of wheat to run five quarters (22½ cwt) to the acre. Last year my wheat averaged nearly double the yield of that single outstanding crop: the same farm, mind you, and the same farmer. I know there are many reasons for this – better varieties to stand up to heavier use of fertilisers, smaller field losses with a combine-harvester and so on – but certainly chemicals to control weeds and insect pests have helped. When these came on the market we farmers thought they were just our meal-ticket. We were being exhorted day in, day out to become more efficient; and looking at it more broadly, human population was in a state of world-wide explosion, and dire were the prophecies of famine to come. Here was the answer, we thought.

Just how short-sighted we were in our optimism is indicated by Rachel Carson in *Silent Spring* (Hamilton, 25s). With a wealth of detail backed by 47 pages of references to the literature, she describes the many unforeseen side-effects. Mammals, birds, fish, bees and other beneficial insects – all have been killed, often in massive numbers, at some time and in some place. And in two horrific chapters she shows the potential threat to human health through mutations in our genes and cancer. The two most dangerous groups, both insecticides, are the chlorinated hydrocarbons (DDT, dieldrin, aldrin, heptachlor and BHC) and organic phosphates (parathion and malathion). The former particularly are persistent and not excreted, so they build up in the body; and even a sub-lethal dose may reduce fertility. One chemical may react with another and trigger off the deadliness of either. Moreover insects have shown astonishing powers of developing resistant strains, so that within a few years their numbers may actually increase, since spraying has become ineffective and their natural predators have been reduced. The central message of the book is the folly of attacking a single organism without considering the total complex of its environment. Biological problems demand biological solutions; and the author gives many examples of successful biological control in its widest sense, where due account has been taken of the ecology of the pest species …

What are the lessons for us in Britain? Already we have warning signs. The virtual disappearance of the sparrowhawk from eastern and southern England and the scarcity of some once common butterflies are only two … Miss Carson does not say much about weedkillers, but what of their effects on food-chains: weeds–insects–birds? In the meantime what should farmers, growers and, not least important, gardeners do? …

Some people may feel that the book is alarmist and fails to take proper account of the real benefits these chemicals have brought in increased food production and control of human and animal diseases. Its value lies in the warning it gives; we are playing with new powers whose results we have neglected to calculate. It makes far from hilarious reading, but it merits the attention of everyone who has the future of our wild life, and indeed of his own species, at heart. *R.K. Cornwallis*

Roads and Lanes

by R.H. Grenville

Roads are always mindful of a purpose,
Have places and objectives on their mind.
Lanes are like a dreamer's thoughts, like love
That reaches in no certainty to find,
But full of quiet hope. Roads are impatient
With inefficiency. Lanes love to wind.

Roads stream across the continent and race
By bridge and tunnel to their journey's end,
Speeding the restless millions on their way.
But lanes go sauntering along the bend
Of streams you know; in places you remember
With poignant love, await you like a friend.

LISTENING IN

Our Dorset gardener had an infallible and, I believe, unique method of diagnosing the condition of our cat, Lucy. Holding her in his arms, he would shake her with gentle vigour against his ear. A moment of hushed expectancy: then, with solemn assurance, he would pronounce her either 'full' or 'empty'. Eventually came a day when he declared Lucy to be 'full, but not very full'. One kitten resulted.   *Isobel St. Vincent*

1964

Le Nouveau Camping

BY BRUCE CAMPBELL

A 1934 design for le nouveau camping – plus car.

The first night I slept out in a car was on the slopes of Skirrid Fawr near Abergavenny. I occupied the passenger seat of a small open two-seater and was extremely uncomfortable. Our rest, such as it was, terminated when the driver somehow released the brake in his troubled sleep, and we started to run backwards down a steep lane. At this period, more than thirty years ago, a family camping holiday with car involved typically a series of Laocoön-like struggles with an ex-army bell tent, which in transit filled the boot or bulged precariously on the roof-rack. To most people the idea that the car and the tent could have anything to say to each other was a long time coming; indeed, as late as 1958 diehards like us were still fighting away with a bell tent on the shores of Lough Currane.

Then the revolution overtook us and, three years later, the calmer waters of Morbihan saw us cooking on a calor-gas unit which rested on the tailboard of an estate car under the awning of a two-chambered Continental tent – one of thousands of families who had at last realised that camping, instead of an annual exercise in the sterner virtues, could be labour-saving and comfortable without any loss of freedom and enjoyment.

… Attempts to mate the car and the tent have a surprisingly long history, back to 1934 when they were connected by an awning which allowed undercover access from one to the other; the porch of the modern frame tent carries on this idea.

Two recent designs locate the folded tent on the roof-rack. In one, costing about £50, the rack is the frame, from which telescopic legs protrude. When they have reached the ground, the rack is unscrewed from the car, the leg joints are fully extended and the car is driven away, leaving a typical frame tent behind … The second design … provides smallish sleeping tent for two on the roof of the car in a matter of seconds. It overhangs and is reached by a metal ladder.

1965

One Countryman to Another
TOWN AND COUNTRY

THREE DECISIONS OF THE Minister of Housing and Local Government to allow extensive building in the proposed green belts round London, Birmingham and Sheffield brought into the open an issue that can be evaded no longer: how, in the immediate as well as in the more distant future, are we to provide for an 'exploding' population equipped with the motor car, marrying earlier and less inclined than previous generations to share accommodation? A second round of new towns, more ambitious than any so far built, is already on the way; and interim plans have been announced for the South-East. But final decisions will now have to await the completion of other regional studies. At best they can bring no relief until the 1970s. Even some new or expanded towns already designated – Dawley, for example, and Redditch – will give little return in the next three years. Meanwhile the pressure is, in Mr. Crossman's own words, enormous and terrifying. He sees as the greatest danger for large tracts of rural England the process of 'seepage' – piecemeal development of perhaps a field or two here and there – which may destroy the intimate, closely integrated character of dozens more villages, as it has already done within forty

or fifty miles of the overflowing cities.

It is fortunate that Mr. Crossman lives in a village in north Oxfordshire and knows the problems at first hand, for he has declared his determination to make personally the decisions that are constitutionally his; and no-one who has experienced his strong and vigorous personality would expect otherwise. He sees himself as holding the line, especially of the two actual and many proposed green belts, against immense pressure until a long-term strategy can emerge. At the same time he is acutely aware of another of his responsibilities, to see that slum clearance and the building of new houses are at no time held up for lack of sites ...

The extent of the pressure on green belts is partly due to the falsification of earlier population forecasts and the time taken to adjust such plans as did exist. But it is also directed there because so little has been done to enable people to see the positive merits of a green belt ... Generally, the purpose of a green belt has been defined as to make the country way of life accessible to those who live in big cities. They will also look increasingly for specialised facilities there.

> " *The South-Eastern Electricity Board seem to be getting into the rural way of life. Witness a 'Wanted' ad. in a copy of the* West Sussex Gazette *sent to us by Hilda E. Young: 'Shorthorn typist for small typing section'.* "

1966

How The Farmer Sees It

BY TRISTRAM BERESFORD

The author, who farms with partners at Chilmark in Wiltshire, has farmed also on the Isle of Wight, in Wales and in Somerset. He was for ten years a member of the Hill Farming Research Organisation with three hill farms in Scotland, and for a longer period agricultural correspondent of the Financial Times. *He is now a member of the Nature Conservancy for England and of the South West Economic Planning Council.*

Working late on our grain-drier, you see the traffic on A303 at the top of the farm. When the wind is from the north you hear it too, though it is a mile or more away. It goes on all night: west to Cornwall, east to London, mostly cars but some heavy lorries too. Two hundred miles farther west, at a roadside café beyond Truro, you will hear the same sound – whish ... whish – as the cars flash past, and wonder what happens to all these countless vehicles when they reach their Land's End. How can there be room for them all on the dwindling Cornish peninsula? They say that tourism in Devon and Cornwall is worth £100m. a year, more than the gross output of agriculture and horticulture in those two counties combined; and income from tourism is rising. In five years' time it will be £200m. according to the planners. But by that time the roads to the West will be choked solid.

Watching the headlights on A303 at night, you are aware of so much more than holiday traffic: not just the urge people have to get away, but the strange new phenomenon of urban stress that drives them to the seaside in unprecedented numbers for the momentary relief of a wider horizon, or drives them, mostly westwards, in search of those vanishing luxuries – space, privacy, fresh air, peace. The more leisure we have, the more pressing will be our need for them, the more we shall resent the constriction of our roads – narrow corridors bounded by fences, banks and hedgerows – the more we shall want to get out and cut the barbed wire. How are we, farmers and landowners, likely to fare when these stresses build up, as they seem bound to do? Britain is the only nation in the world with a population of 50m. that has less than 5 per cent of its working population engaged in agriculture; in 1970 we shall be 4 per cent. But we are virtually the only members of the population who enjoy space, privacy, fresh air, peace or anything like it.

We occupy four-fifths of the land area, and we are so thin on the ground that, if we were spread evenly over the landscape, we would be out of earshot of one another. Townspeople, on the other hand, are so penned in that, metaphorically speaking, they cannot move without treading on each other's toes.

… Held up by a herd of cows on a main road, I started to figure. There were 51 of them, black-and-white, all good milkers by their bags. Put them in at £100 apiece and you had a capital asset of more than £5,000. Each animal would be good for five lactations at 900 gallons, reckoning no more than average performance, plus, say, four calves. Adding it up, here was a property that would turn over £40,000–£50,000 in its working life. Why, I wonder, are we impatient sometimes when halted by cattle, yet respectful when stopped by police to make way for a tank transporter? Of the two, herd or tank, there is no doubt which is the more pleasing and productive asset.

" On a quiet road in north Buckinghamshire I suspected engine trouble and drew into a lay-by. I had had my head under the bonnet of my 1964 Austin A40 only a matter of seconds when another motorist pulled up, jumped out and said, 'It's all right, mate. You can have the battery. I'm only taking the wheels.' " R.C. Horwood

---

COUNTRYMAN CLUB

RAILWAY MANNERS

Fifty years ago, Tom Holton told me, his father was station-master at Towcester and the family lived in the station house. When Tom's little sister died in an epidemic, the railway company put on a special train to carry the coffin and mourners to their ancestral home at the village of Slapton five miles away. The train waited at the nearest point to the church while bearers carried the coffin half a mile along a field path to the churchyard and the burial took place. The track was a single line, so no other train could pass. The family were then conveyed back to Towcester. The company, the Stratford-upon-Avon and Midland Junction Railway, was more than once in the receiver's hands, but it was not too poor to pay this compliment to a faithful servant. *C.E. Goshawk, Northants*

UNDER-FLOOR HEATING

At the old free gospel chapel at Briscoe, near Ronaldkirk in Teesdale, the upper floor housed the room used for worship: sheep were let into the ground-floor room before a service to warm the building.
Geoffrey N. Wright, Somerset

GLEANINGS FROM SHEEP STREET

A GLOUCESTERSHIRE READER tells us of a local farmer who bought a dozen turkeys to fatten for the Christmas market. Within a fortnight half of them had committed suicide by stretching their own necks after putting their heads through the wire netting of the pen. He opened the door and left the remaining birds to roam the yard, where they took up positions in a row along the top of a water tank. Later in the day a car backfired and so surprised them that four fell into the water and were drowned. At the New Year the farmer made no secret of his resolution to stick to cockerels next Christmas.

" Two small boys were boasting in the lane about their dads. Jimmy, aggressively: 'My dad's got a lot of cows, an' he's got a bull down in the meadow by the stream.' Alec, scornfully: 'My dad's got a hullaballoo in the rick yard; he said so this morning.' " Janet Norton

As It Seems to Some of Us
TIME FOR A GESTURE

THE MINISTRY OF DEFENCE, as Rodney Legg reminds us, is one of the largest landowners south of the Thames. It clings to acres occupied in war-time, all pledges to civilians long since forgotten. He has in mind several miles of rugged cliff east of Lulworth Cove, the broad sweep of Worbarrow Bay, heath land stretching towards Poole Harbour and, in a hollow of the Purbeck Hills, the little village of Tyneham – a cluster of stone cottages, a boarded-up church and an Elizabethan manor-house, where life stopped abruptly in 1943. When the large noticeboard pledging the return of the land disappeared after the war, the place was showered with shells; but there is another aspect of its fate.

No caravan camp perches on the cliffs at Worbarrow; no red-brick bungalow bridges a gap between storm-beaten cottages. In spring the downs are painted with bluebells; deer have moved into the woods; sea birds flourish along the cliffs; buzzards and other birds of prey can still be seen there. In May it will be twenty-one years since the war in Europe ended. What could be more timely than a visit by the Prime Minister to Tyneham to hand this superb stretch of coastline over to the National Trust? It would be a dramatic gesture. And what a grand start to the round of regional conferences on coastal preservation which the National Parks Commission are to hold from May onwards!

> *" When I asked a gardening friend whether he was much troubled by birds, he said that they came from all over the place: 'But I've done 'em,' he went on. 'I sowed me peas late one night an' pretended to be doin' it at t'other end o' the garden next mornin'. Birds was all watchin', an' soon as I'd sticked they was down. They've bin scrattin' for a fortnight an' found nowt yet.'))* E.A.C. Husbands, Notts

1967

READERS' MOTORING TALES

On a hot summer's day in 1911 our Tin Lizzie found the Dorset hills steep and climbed them backwards, the reverse being lower than the first forward gear. The water boiled, and a telltale drip-drip suggested a leaking radiator. In a small market town we found a garage – a rarity in those days. 'Try this,' said the proprietor, putting a handful of oatmeal into the radiator; 'that'll swell like porridge and seal the leak.' And it did. *May Hankey*

'There was even sanitation—out in the garden, of course.'

The outdoor privy, in a 1967 article by Jennifer Jarvis about the tied cottage that went with her husband's job as head gardener in the 1930s.

Horseshoes through the ages: (above) *late Celtic, 11th–16th cent., Tudor to early 17th cent.;*
(below) *17th cent,. 17th–18th cent., 19th cent. onwards*

*MERL (the Museum of English Rural Life, based in Reading) ran a long series
in which readers were invited to submit 'curious' objects. In the spring of 1967 this
included a piece on dating ancient horseshoes.*

*" Yorkshire farmer, looking over machinery at auction sale:
'There's more sore arses than sore 'ands these days.' "*

*" Cornish weather prophet, well over ninety:
'You've got to 'ave March. You mayn't get it till
June, but you've got to 'ave it.' "*

METHOD IN MADNESS

OLD GEORGE WAS a carter in the Manhood, the extensive wheat-growing district of Selsey in Sussex. He was very ancient when I knew him in the 1920s. I remember him dressed always in a smock and bowler hat; occasionally a hare or partridge dangled from his belt. Every summer a crop of wheat appeared on the thatch of his cottage. It kept the birds busy, he said, and they were better there than on the peas. When the wheat ripened he put his hens on the roof 'to clean it up a bit'. Indoors the roots hung in festoons, and Old George had to wear his bowler in bed 'to keep the rain off'. Fortunately it hardly ever did rain in that district in summer; there was only the sea mist drifting inland. When the thatch finally rotted and fell in, Old George pushed it into one room which he used as the 'broody house' for chick rearing. He rethatched the cottage himself in the evenings after work.
J. Scott Pitcher

As One Countryman to Another

BY WHAT WILL THOSE who care for the future of our countryside remember 1967? It opened still under the cloud of Aberfan, a tragedy due to the grossest sort of landscape spoliation. It saw the wreck of the 'Torrey Canyon', after which the beaches of Cornwall suffered, and the whole South Coast was threatened by, unparalleled oil pollution. For marine life, cure by detergents proved worse than the disease. Then we were told that architects were planning the biggest ever oil-tanker. It was the year when the battle for the Upper Teesdale reservoir ended, and the victors felt impelled to offer £100,000 for research to mitigate the damage that will be done to a unique flora; when one Act of Parliament encouraged farmers to fill in their ponds, and another gave added protection to our birds; when threats to one of the last unspoiled treasure-houses of nature, the remote island of Aldabra in the Indian Ocean, grew for defence reasons that were incomprehensible to many.

There were conferences of all kinds dealing with aspects of this crisis of the environment: from the landscaping of motorways to the part youth can play internationally in meeting its challenge. An optimistic book by an agricultural economist made the case for a planned use of the world's land resources that could take care of the worst the population explosion might achieve. Another, by a science writer, suggested that men should forsake the power game in favour of the useful and innocuous 'environment game'. A third, by a zoologist, restated with gusto man's origins and described the simian instincts which his intellect may not be able to control. Two others ... looked soberly at the problem, with special emphasis on the effects of the pollution all around us. One of the biggest manufacturers of agricultural chemicals sponsored more delightful records of bird song. No doubt someone somewhere, engaged in scarifying the scenery, put one of his bulldozers out of action because a blackbird had built her nest in it. The human situation is full of such anomalies; without them it would be a poor look-out for writers and dramatists. What matters is the balance of advantage: are there signs that more people are recognising the urgency of the crisis and are prepared to do something about it? ... Have we to wait for some colossal disaster before the still small voices of conservation can make themselves heard on aspects of major policy? ... The need now is to put a price on 'the power of the wilderness'. Only thus will pragmatists be convinced that the modern technological society cannot function efficiently without its balm.

" Gardener, describing local teenager: 'She 'ad a skirt so short you couldn't 'ardly see it an' 'er 'air over 'er eyes, all bits an' bats. Looked like a cabbage gone to seed – all leggy.' "

Bluebell Time

by Arnold Wiles

'That's good blubells you've ruined!'

'Forgot to shut the gate.'

'So glad you like my bluebells. I'm partial to tulips myself.'

1968–1977

Agribusiness Versus the Home Acre

The 1970s were known for the 'small is beautiful' and self-sufficiency movements, when some country dwellers (usually from the towns) began to hark back to the simpler life, seeing themselves as modern peasants in contrast to the big business that agriculture had generally become. The 'conscience' themes of conservation, pollution and concern for the environment in general continued. Pylons, new motorways and bypasses were often viewed with alarm for their intrusion in the landscape.

Major impacts in this period included a rapid rise in house prices, loss of hedgerows, the spread of Dutch elm disease, the strikes and power cuts of 1974, and the great drought of the summer of 1976. Oh, and that little thing called the EEC – the European Economic Community …

This was probably the period in which the general public began to turn against farmers and express indignation at what many saw as 'depredation' in the countryside. By now, too, there had been a marked decline in the influence of the landed gentry: ever since the departure of Robertson Scott as editor two decades earlier, their voices had been growing fainter in its pages.

New regular writers in the journal included Lawrence D. Hills, Hew Watt (who replaced Tristram Beresford as a farming voice) and Rosemary Verey in the garden. In the summer of 1971, after serving for 24 years, John Cripps retired from the editorship and handed over to Devon journalist Crispin Gill, who settled comfortably into his ten-year stint. And in 1977 *The Countryman* celebrated its 50th birthday with full-colour artwork on its cover.

In the meantime decimalisation of the currency confused readers when shillings and pence became 'new pee' and the price of the journal became 30p instead of six shillings in the spring of 1971. This had increased to 50p (ten shillings) by the winter of 1978 – four times the original price and double what it had been in 1961. It was a sign of the times.

1968

As a Farmer Sees It

BY TRISTRAM BERESFORD

To my way of thinking, a system of farming becomes objectionable or worse when it ceases to be congruous, ordinate, just. I would argue, like the eighteenth-century Quaker John Woolman, that man is given government over creatures and lesser orders of creation including plants and soil, and that it is his responsibility to govern justly, ordinately, with congruity, and not to exploit. Exploitation is not government, but despotism. The harm despotism does to any form of life is unquestionable, but the harm is secondary to the damage done to the despot – man himself – and to the society of which he is member. It is for this reason that society steps in to protect itself.

What is offensive in the man who exploits his livestock, or for that matter in the customer who buys the end-product, is lack of sensibility. Abuse of nature is possible only if we coarsen our sensibilities. Here we come back to Schweitzer's fundamental principle of reverence for life, which is something deeply engrained in us, and not only in Western man. The North American Indian fulfilled a small rite of gratitude to the deer he killed. He distributed its entrails to other living things. He needed the deer to live; he took the deer, but he exalted his own spirit in the way he did it. The Maya hunter did the same. In all, humility; grace before meat; the religious approach, the recognition of kinship, of congruity with all forms of life.

Not only are such thoughts part of the wisdom of the race: the experience from which they derive is perennial too. There are, without our always allowing for them, checks and balances built into our human ecosystem; a scrupulous accountancy, minutely at work; an infallible reckoning that always in the end corrects our marginal miscalculations and is sometimes called the swing of the pendulum. These checks and balances – I call them regulators – remind us that, though we have great freedom, we remain captive. They make their appearances, show their warning signs, whenever we attempt to move too fast, without prudence, without justice or against our better judgment, as we say. They tell us that it takes time to produce character or sound timber or even a good steak. We have nature's word for it that our too prolific strawberries lack taste. The overcrowding of animals gives rise to epidemics. An insufficiently tested drug produces thalidomide babies …

Progress has to be made slowly, with circumspection. Hunches have to stand the test of experience, and experience is one of the few things we cannot prefabricate. The Greeks knew this and called the sin against experience *hubris*. It was the pride that comes before a fall.

'We hardly notice it'

The Natural History of Words

BY BRUCE CAMPBELL

… One last word of honourable mention is 'jizz', which to bird-watchers means what sailors are supposed to call 'the cut of his jib', the indefinable specific way in which a wood sandpiper looks slightly different from a green sandpiper even in silhouette. It came into natural history some time before 1922 in a newspaper article by T.A. Coward. This began: 'A West Coast Irishman was familiar with wild creatures which dwelt on or visited his rocks and shores; at a glance he could name them, usually correctly, but if asked how he knew them would reply,

"By their jizz"'. Later Coward defined it as 'character rather than characteristics, the *tout ensemble* of the subject'. He was not sure of its spelling, or even that it had been written down before. When in Ireland a few years ago I started a hunt after its origins. I cannot find it in a dialect dictionary, but forms of it are in general use; all suggest liveliness, of a young man's nature or a motor-car's engine: 'Jizz her up, man!' My own hunch is that it is the parent of 'jazz', and thus a key word of our curious century which has seen both bird-watching and pop music become world-wide cults.

COUNTRYMAN CLUB

GUINEA-PIG

At Belay near Caernarvon some years ago I saw a foot-high fence of wire netting being pegged neatly across a lawn, enclosing about 100 white guinea-pigs. The ex-batman gardener told me that his ex-officer employer disliked the noise of lawn-mowers. The guinea-pigs made a good job of the grass: seven days, seven moves, then start again. During the winter they were confined to barracks on a diet of bran mash, and the surplus young were sold to defray expenses.   *Dorothy Hartley, Denbighshire*

1969

COUNTRYMAN CLUB

DOWN THE WELL

My cousin, Miss Lefevre, was recently visited by a workman who had just finished filling in an old well in the garden of the house in Whittlesey, Northants, where she was born. In the well he had found a sealed glass bottle containing the following message written by her grandfather, who originally owned the property: 'June 4th 1881. The well top having fallen in was this day removed and well thoroughly cleaned out, pumped dry etc., by Wm Parratt in the employ of Jno Fevre'. There followed a list of the members of the family, ten of them from John Fevre, born 1812, and his wife Marian down to Ellen, aged 12 weeks; the six elder children had signed their names and Marian, aged two, made her mark. Then this admission: 'My wife, who would like to wear the breeches (but wont) says I am to add that the well fell in nine months ago and this is a specimen of my promptness in attending to business. It was to be done one week after another, but always put off but at last it is finished. Whoever takes this out of the bottle, if after 20 years, may go to the nearest Hotel and have a pint of best ale and if living I will pay for it.' My cousin was very willing to honour her grandfather's bargain, but the workman declined the ale with thanks, being a teetotaller.

Leonard Taylor, Somerset

HAY-FEVER CURE

For 40 years I had had 50 inoculations every spring and still suffered from hay fever. Three years ago, seeing an advertisement in *The Countryman* for Spanish orange blossom honey, I sent for some and started to take it at every meal, eating about 1lb. a week from November to April. Since then I have not had a single sneeze nor any other hay-fever symptom, and I intend to continue the treatment as long as I live. I was 85 in March. Australian Medium Amber honey is equally effective and has an excellent flavour. I also take a teaspoonful of cider vinegar three times daily.

Alice E. Tyssen-Gee, Surrey

" Countrywoman, asked the ages of her four children: 'I got one lap baby, one crawler, one porch child an' one yard young 'un.' "

AGRIBUSINESS VERSUS THE HOME ACRE (1968–1977) **129**

These Byways Are Inhabited

BY H.F. ELLIS

A while ago there was a mild agitation ... for a national Courtesy Week on the roads ... The idea behind such weeks must be that everyone will discover what a nice change it makes and continue in the same for months and years thereafter. What actually happens is that the courteous remain courteous, some few make an ironical parade of the business, taking off their hats and bowing to pedestrians at uncontrolled crossings, and the rest seize such mean advantages as they can and push on ...

What did interest me, during the discussions about this Courtesy Week in the newspaper that mooted the plan, was a particularly bland observation (presently to be awarded italics) by one writer on the misbehaviour of local motorists and tractor drivers. He had been quoting some woman correspondent's complaint that men drivers would rarely pull up to let a car out of a side road in the rush hour, and he went on:

> This, I feel, is hardly fair. Most drivers on a major road are prepared to let a car pull out in front of them, if only because one more does not make all that difference. Conversely, one of

the worst offenders against good motoring manners on the open road *is the local motorist who pulls out in front of through traffic, and then dawdles along for a hundred yards or so before turning off again.*

Here, unless I gravely misrepresent his attitude, speaks the representative of that great black cloud of motorists who really think that the long-distance driver, en route for Rhyl with bucket and spade or Aberystwyth with samples of crockery, has some kind of superior importance; that through traffic has, or ought to have, the status of an express train, at whose imperious approach the local riff-raff should cower in sidings like so many coal trains or cheap Wednesday excursions. We who live in the country take a different view. It is true that when we ourselves, once in a while, undertake a journey of some magnitude, something of the same long-distance arrogance may come upon us as we sweep into countrysides and country townships other than our own. It may then seem pretty intolerable that we, who face the immense task of getting to Doncaster by nightfall, should be inconvenienced by a man whose only aim, after pulling out of Willoughby

Road, is to turn up Millstone Lane. But we stop short of aggrandising an irrational impatience into a divine right.

The plain fact is that the local driver has work to do, or pleasure to enjoy, not at all less important to him – and perhaps even to the welfare of the state – than the business or pleasure of the long-distance motorist. The tractor driver turns into the 'open road' (whatever that may mean) and off it again, because that is the way from A to B. He is not to be blamed if the distance is only a hundred yards; indeed you might have thought the following motorists would be glad it was no more. And as for 'dawdling along', it ought to be understood that tractors are not equipped to cruise at sixty m.p.h. ... If these simple facts are not clear to motoring correspondents, some of them had better take time

off from road-testing Jaguars and try out a Massey Ferguson with a load of mangels in tow.

The point to be remembered, by any long-distance motorists who may be brooding on courtesy as they hew a path through my part of the countryside, is that we who get in their way are at least within our own bailiwick. We live here ... In our eyes the traffic that streams through *en route* for somewhere else has no superior status whatever. On the contrary: strangers, intruders, second-class citizens, that is what you are. We realise that you have no option, and that you will be as glad as we shall be when the motorway is ready to isolate you in a land where no tractors dawdle and nobody turns left or right from dawn to sunset. But in the meantime kindly remember that you are here on sufferance, and mind your manners.

1970

Riding the Bore

When I was seventeen my mother sent me on an errand from Blakeney to Slimbridge; and to save time I took my bicycle with me on the ferry from Newnham. For the old ferryman this meant two trips to the boat, first with me on his back and then with the bicycle, over the stretch of mud left by the receding tide, and two more trips on the other side. He told me I must be back within two hours; but I was several minutes late and found the tide at its lowest with only a narrow stretch of water on the Newnham side. The ferryman, in some excitement, took me on his back again and, dragging my bicycle with him, hurried across the now wide stretch of mud to the boat, which he pulled away in haste. After the first few strokes of his oars he sat still and leaned forward listening. "'Tis the bore,' he said. 'Too risky getting ye ashore now. 'Im be 'ere an' 'im'll be a big un. Just sit still in the middle o' the boat an' 'old on.' He stood up, planted his feet well apart, placed his oars deeply in the water and faced the oncoming wave. There was a distant rumble like an approaching train; then a wall of rushing water came surging round the horseshoe bend. The bore was a moderate one, probably not more than five feet high, but awe-inspiring enough from my position in a small rowing boat in mid stream. Suddenly it was upon us with a roar. The bow of the boat seemed to leap upwards and we swayed violently; but the ferryman knew his job and kept the little craft head on. I was thankful when he could resume his seat and swing round for the shore. As we reached it he remarked, 'Don't recall ever 'avin' anybody in me boat afore when the bore come. But I usually goes out on me own to meet 'im.'

Eric F. Powell

Fetch a Leet

BY DORA A. COLE

A farmer friend joined us in the byre as we were tying up the cows in their new places for the winter and listening to their contented crunching of crisp clean hay. 'There's a bonny laal Shorthorn,' he said, looking at Peggy; 'she puts me i' mind of a coo we had at Calebeck. Coos had been oot at grass, an' when Ah fetched 'em in, this un Ah's tellin' ye aboot niver offered t' eat her hay. She just stood an' looked at it. Ah couldn't see owt wrang wid her an' nor could Mother.

'Geordie Crosby was gannin' wid oor Maggie at time, an' he's a gey good hand amang t' cattle. When he cam' across he looked at oor coo an' he was just aboot baffled. Then he says, "Ah'll just have a look at her teeth." He put his hand in her mooth an' fumbled aboot a bit, an' then he says, "By Gox, fetch a leet! Ah believe she has nae tongue."

'We got a leet an' sure enough, she had lost her tongue. There was nowt but a stump left an' it looked gey sore. "Ah'll tell tha what," said Geordie.

"She'll ha getten it catched in yan o' them eire snarles. Chaps poachin' aboot fields wid them snarles should be hanged wid 'em thersells."

'She was a good laal coo in milk, but hoo t' keep her up we didn't know. All we could do was give her calf gruel for the time. Then one day Ah was sittin' beside her, wonderin' hoo t' get some hay intil her, when Ah hit on the idea o' makin' laal balls o' hay an' shovin' them intil her mooth. She liked it, an' it got her on chewin' her cud again. Ah kept on makin' them balls every time Ah could spare a minute – in me dinner oor, at tea time an' when Ah was finished at neet – an' she soon got t' openin' her mooth an' waitin' o' me pushin' them in.

'After a few weeks her stump of a tongue got healed up an' she started tryin' t' get hay intil her mooth hersel', an' after a while langer she managed it an' was feedin' hersel' again. We kept her many a year, an' nobbut us ever knew she had nobbut half a tongue.'

Orchard Roundabout

by D. Macer Wright

When our orchard was planted in the mid 'thirties an oak dying from honey fungus (*Armillaria mellea)* was removed, and a space judged adequate was left all round it. The tenacity of this fungus was under-estimated. Since then more than twenty trees have succumbed, and I am still digging out victims. The latest showed no black rhizomorphs or 'bootlaces', and I tried to convince myself that death was due to some other cause. But the fan-like pattern of the white mycelium beneath dead root-bark and its fleshy nature, easily seen under a lens, left little doubt. I took samples away for what I call the glow-worm test. After dark these showed the luminous glow that confirms *Armillaria*. Not all pieces necessarily glow, so several are needed.

> *Advice from a gardener in Kent: 'If you want to get rid of your fingers and toes, dig in all your dentures. Helps keep off the dolphin too.' [To get rid of club root, dig in bonfire ash. Wards off black fly too. To densher or Devonshire is to cut turf from pasture land and burn it to ashes.]*

*'To advertise a pop festival **and** let your bull into the field was wrong.'*

Coming to Terms with The Environment

YEARS AGO, WHEN my own environment was a play-pen, or its Edwardian equivalent, with a couple of small flannel waistcoats airing on one side of it, there was a general belief that every organism had its environment and was affected by it. Moths had one, and became noticeably melanistic if there was a lot of soot about. At this time, too, heredity was a word much bandied about outside the confines of my nursery. Some said that inherited characteristics were more influential and enduring than those developed in and by an individual's surroundings; others said not.

Just when the environment got its definite article I am unable to say. It must have been round about the time that facilities and amenities began to spring up and proliferate in this already overcrowded island. Facilities for recreation, reading, worship, washing and so on took the place of old-fashioned football grounds, libraries, churches etc., and very soon began to group themselves into Amenities by a process akin, it may be, to osmosis. For a man already far gone in middle age it was not easy to adjust to these ameliorations. The concept of adjustment itself was hardly more than embryonic in my formative years. My old nurse, for instance, when she made some irksome change in my environment (a sailor suit, perhaps), never included 'You must learn to adjust to new pressures, Master H.' among her innumerable wise saws and encouraging maxims. Still, I made some attempt as time went by to bring order and method into a situation of increasing complexity and actually got to work on the construction of a kind of statistical table ... If this scheme had gained general acceptance it might have done something to keep the growth of the Environment within bounds.

There was also an infestation at about this time of Neighbourhoods, Precincts (hitherto only encountered in stories about New York cops) and Vertically Integrated Concepts, which were difficult to fit into any comprehensive numerical scheme. Heredity remained reasonably constant, but with the Environment it was becoming daily more arduous to keep in touch. Offshore rigs, to my astonishment, were sunk in it, and to evaluate the influence of these tripods on my characteristics, as compared with my father's genes, was entirely beyond my compass ...

Meanwhile the Environment was growing apace. By 1969 it had utterly abandoned its old role of blackening the wings of moths and was now conterminous with the British Isles and their surrounding seas. By 1970 it was lapping the shores of the United States. Inevitably, instead of influencing others it became itself subject to almost intolerable pressures ... The boot was now on the other leg with a vengeance. With its mastery over human and animal life almost entirely gone, the Environment had become something to be saved, and the British Government, in what looked like a last desperate throw, appointed a Secretary of State for it.   *H.F. Ellis*

Progress Without Pollution

The Prime Minister [Edward Heath]

It is the great paradox of our time that as man's inventive genius carries him nearer and nearer to the stars he should suddenly be forced to pause and take stock of what is happening to his environment on earth.

The greatest problem facing this generation is to leave behind a world fit to live in. International discussion and co-operation on environmental matters are already taking place, and the United Nations are to stage a Conference on the Human Environment in Stockholm next year. The nations of the world are beginning to take this challenge seriously.

Britain is a leader in this. We are the first country in the world to have created a single Department with all the powers and the resources needed to devise and carry out a fully comprehensive policy to protect and improve our environment.

Britain is a small densely populated island. Land available to us for expansion and development is restricted on all sides by the sea. It is therefore vitally important that we should strike the right balance between the needs of conservation and development while safeguarding our countryside and combating all forms of pollution. This is why, in our reorganisation of the machinery of Government, the Department of the Environment became responsible not simply for the control and containment of pollution, but for all the functions of land-use planning including all major services in the field of housing and new town development, water resources, regional development, road planning and the entire transport infrastructure.

We are largely and increasingly an urban civilisation, and it is our urban development that is in greatest need of repair. The priority we give to the renewal of our towns and cities, where most of our people live, is obviously right and proper. But town and country are now so closely inter-linked that the need for redevelopment within the urban areas is bound to threaten the open country. What we have to do is find a means of solving urban problems without, in the process, damaging the face and, perhaps even more important, the nature of the rural scene. The real danger to the countryside is not the conflict between amenity and development, but the neglect of one through bad management of the other.

The beauty of our countryside must be assured. But I believe this will be achieved not through a sterile policy of preservation in the narrowest defensive sense, but by proper planning and management of all our resources. We have made a beginning.

1972

What Should We Do About Pollution

IAN NAIRN, JOURNALIST. Stop breeding like bloody rabbits, stop using more than you need to, stop lusting after power, stop lusting after possessions whether they are persons or slices of the land surface, stop making more of a profit than you need to enjoy yourself, stop working by the rule book, precedent and what the neighbours might say. And start loving the landscape and townscape for its own sweet sake. In other words, a spiritual revolution to match our technological revolution.

J.B. PRIESTLEY, AUTHOR AND PLAYWRIGHT. I can only suggest the following priority list:
1. The Air. We have gone some way to clearing the air of smoke etc., but we obviously have not gone far enough. We should prepare to have fewer and not more motor cars in the near future, and all very large lorries should be banned altogether.
2. Rivers, if only because so many of them move through large centres of population. I am certain a great deal could be done here.
3. The Sea Coast.
Men responsible for persistent pollution, who have been given several warnings, should not be fined but sent to prison.

PROFESSOR ARNOLD TOYNBEE, HISTORIAN. My personal order of priority of urgency for conserving and improving the environment is:
1. To stop polluting, and then to re-purify, the streams, rivers, lakes, and the sea.
2. To save the air from being polluted by the emission of fumes from petrol-driven road vehicles and planes.
3. To abate the noise produced by mechanisation.
4. To reduce congestion of road traffic.
My point (3) would be partly achieved by progress towards (2). For (2) and (4) I should like to see a reversion from petrol-driven road-traffic to electricity-driven rail-traffic, and a substitution of electricity for petrol in the necessary minimum of road-vehicles.
I should like to see fumeless planes made compulsory, if this is technically possible. If it is not, I should like to see a limitation on the number of planes allowed to operate.

Wild Life and Tame

COLONISTS IN CROYDON

It was in the late summer of 1970 that I first noticed an unusual visitor to the Shirley area of Croydon in the form of a beautifully coloured but noisy parakeet, and assumed that it had escaped from a local aviary. The winter of 1970–71 was relatively mild and by the late spring or early summer of 1971 the parakeet population had considerably increased; I had definitely seen nine birds in flight or perched on trees and a neighbour confirmed sighting 11. There appeared to be a decline early this year, but on 21 May I saw five in flight and eight passed over in close formation on 16 July. Their flight is very swift and low, and the birds invariably utter raucous cries when on the wing. They have catholic tastes in food, embracing berries, bread and other food scraps and, regrettably, the fruit in local gardens and even the buds on my magnolia. Nevertheless they are so delightful and unique that the odd apple or pear is a small price to pay for their well-being and to keep them with us. – F.C.W. Wheatley, Surrey.

[R.C. Homes tells me the breeding of a pair of rose-ringed parakeets, native to Central Africa, at Shirley in 1971 was reported in the Surrey Bird Club Bulletin for Autumn 1971. The birds were seen entering a hole in a beech and later were about with six others, one recently fledged. This total of nine agrees with one of Mr. Wheatley's observations. Provided the winters are not too cold and they have plenty of food, parakeets can survive outside in England. – B.C.]

Somerset farmer: 'Oi've seventy-foive chicks going cheap.'
Friend: 'What do ee expect 'em to do – bark?'

1973

As a Farmer Sees It

by Tristram Beresford

Thoughts on Factory Farming

I watched them coming from the stunner, hanging by their feet from the conveyor line, limp but twitching, throats cut, shedding their blood before they reached the scalding tank and the de-feathering machine on the next stages of their posthumous journey through the processing plant. The sight was obscene; not only on account of the suffering (a few birds survive the stunner) but because of line, posture, the inane curve of head and bill. The corpses had the pathos of the horse's head in Picasso's *Guernica*. It was death without ritual; mechanically administered, mechanically repeated; repeated a hundred million, two hundred million times a year as batch after batch of birds arrived close-packed in crates from the broiler houses after a brief life of fifty days. Alive, they had no dignity. Dead – plucked, drawn, dressed and sheathed in sheer polythene packs – they bloomed in super-markets, wearing labels that evoked the freshness of country life in spring.

I thought of the public benefactors who have pioneered this quick turnover in animal protein. I thought too of the indignities and misery suffered by livestock exported on the hoof – that is to say, alive – to slaughterhouses all over Europe; and of veal calves reared in close confinement on an iron-deficient diet; and of all the cover-up stories, the double-talk, the salesmanship, the propaganda that keeps the housewife in ignorance of the history of what she buys . . . and I thought, there must be something wrong somewhere. Somewhere down the road we have travelled to the present, to the brink of a disintegrating future, we have taken the wrong turning, and would like to find our way back, and start again, and feel we should, but know the cost would be too high.

[Editor's note: This typically thoughtful and level-headed article continues at length with an explanation that the author is not against meat-eating; he is not a vegetarian himself. It is not about whether people should eat meat or not, but about how animals are reared and slaughtered. His plea is against insensibility and exploitation. V.L.P]

Sheep Street Mosaic

A YEAR AGO I was in Stockholm ... for the United Nations Conference on the Environment; it is time for a progress report ... So much we hoped for seems to be at least getting into gear ... Are we going fast enough? Are we eating up our reserves too quickly? Did you see that simple Parliamentary question: 'How long will the world's known oil sources last' and the laconic answer '31 years'? Will all our motor cars stop one afternoon in the year 2004, and all our lights go out?   *Crispin Gill*

Starling-Rise

BY JANE CRESWELL-EVANS

It is mid-December, and I have just realised that we are plagued with starlings.

'Starlings?' said the locals. 'Fire your guns! Beat your drums!' So I pace slowly up and down the drive for an hour at bed-time, beating a ceaseless tom-tom with a pair of baking tins, and uttering shrill yells and shrieks. There is pandemonium among the starlings. Alarmed and bewildered they fly hither and thither, settling and taking off again. A few shots ring out from the direction of the forecourt as my husband joins in, and the starlings that have taken temporary refuge in the pine trees near the houses rise in a dense cloud.

It is dusk now and at last the rhododendrons seem to be deserted. Tired but triumphant I return to the house up the back path. But as I pass behind the bushes that line the drive, suddenly a great multitude of starlings whirrs out from under the leaves! I stop and stare aghast, motionless, incredulous. Is this as far as they have gone?

As I stand the birds, reassured by my silence, return to their perches, and the bed-time twittering resumes. The raw cold wraps me round as I walk on. Every shrub and bush I pass is a-flutter. Throat rasping, feet heavy in their cold rubber boots, fingers stiff and icy clutching irreparably battered tins, I concede the first round to them.

... Earlier than usual one morning I am sitting alone at the table in the window. Suddenly in the rhododendrons a starling flits out from under the leaves and a few feet further on slips in again. Another follows suit, and another. Are they dormitory monitors, perhaps, waking up the sluggards? Group leaders checking on the morning schedules? Or just extroverts paying social calls in their early morning brightness?

All at once a cloud of starlings extricates itself, rising up simultaneously, and flies off. Within seconds another wave follows, and another, and wave after wave, with rhythmic swell, they fly away in every direction. I watch transfixed, marvelling at the number of the birds, the miracle of organisation, and the beauty of their flight …

As peace descends on the garden I feel it also within me. The jangling irritation I felt before slips away, like a heavy and constricting garment

discarded in the sun.

Now I watch also in the evening. The starlings are settling in the dead top of one of the immensely tall pine trees in the garden. Soon every bare branch and twig is laden with birds, so tightly packed it seems as though the dead part of the tree has come to life again … The noise is amazing. They must all be twittering together. Then comes a sudden silence, followed immediately by a loud whirr, as the whole flock, to a bird, takes off simultaneously. Together they fly round and round, in graceful sweeps and swirls. Finally, as though poured from a giant vessel in the sky, they swoop down and vanish behind the bushes bordering the paddock.

'Blue tits in larch'.

1974

Night

BY EDWARD HART

Even countrymen now experience much less of the countryside at night. The car, with its warmth and convenience, insulates us from our nocturnal surroundings. Occasionally fox or deer may be caught in the headlights, but far more is lost.

Former generations journeyed by horse and trap, the clip-clopping of the pony's hooves on stone or sand enhancing rather than obliterating the hoot of the owl or faraway call of a vixen. Or they walked. A cross-country walk at night makes a different world of even the most familiar scene.

… Those who do not know the countryside at night do not know it at all. Because we are unconscious for eight hours at a stretch, we tend to imagine that domestic animals are the same. Yet sheep and cattle graze during part of the night in what seems a more voracious fashion than in daylight. To hear a large flock of sheep nibbling busily as they move steadily over frosted grass is a wonderful sound in the darkness, while the tearings of a herd of dairy cows consuming new ley seem unbelievably loud.

… Not many people would get up at 2 a.m., just to walk in the moonlight, but to return home at that time can be a memorable experience on a lonely farm … Sparkling starlight, the whole dale clearly visible, the beck tinkling in the bottom over its stony bed and every twig and blade of grass rime-encrusted, made a never-to-be-forgotten home-coming.

… Such inexpensive pleasures strike no chord in the urban mind. For this we should be thankful, for there is still plenty of room in the countryside at night.

Candles in Sheep Street

WHEN I JOINED *The Countryman* my old colleagues on *The Western Morning News* very kindly gave me a pair of silver candlesticks: I never expected to be typing with their aid. All this, and a General Election! What has it all been about? A writer in the *Financial Times* saw it as a product of the class struggle that still racks Britain. Some Moscow-watchers maintained that the Russians had for years been urging the Arabs to use oil as a weapon against the Western world. Nearer home we heard all about the Communists and left-wing Socialists dominating the mine-workers.

But, fundamentally, is it not that the warnings of the environmentalists and the conservationists are coming true? We shuddered at the studies that foretold the length of time it would take us to exhaust the known reserves of the earth, and as cheerfully forgot them when other scientists told us the figures were wrong. It could never happen here, we said, just as everyone thinks car crashes or premature deaths only touch other families, not his own. The clever boffins would find fresh sources of energy, we said, forgetting that nuclear fuel has been a quarter of a century coming, and has still not quite made it, and that there was little more life expectancy for oil than that.

Now the sheiks know the scarcity value of their oil. The miners know how precious is their coal. The law of supply and demand is at work. We who feared that man was making his planet uninhabitable never quite worked out how it would happen; what the possible scenarios – to use the current jargon – could be. Perhaps the sheiks and the miners have been showing us the shape of things to come. Power on a few days a week; 50 miles an hour on the roads, thinking twice before taking out the car. American friends report similar tribulations. Are we going to be forced to economise on our use of raw materials by their sheer price? Nothing else seemed to be having any effect. *Crispin Gill*

PIG IN A POKE

A WOMAN FROM New York bought an old farm house in Vermont. Shortly after moving in she asked a neighbouring farmer when the garbage would be collected, but was told there was no such service in the country. 'How do you get rid of your garbage?' enquired the newcomer. The farmer said he fed it to his pigs. 'Would you sell me one?' 'Ayah,' said the Vermonter, and sold her a little pig for ten dollars. The summer passed. The pig grew and grew, and on 1 September the woman sought out the farmer and said as she could not take her pig to New York with her would the farmer buy him back? 'Ayah, if the price is right,' agreed her neighbour. The woman looked thoughtful and said, 'Well, I paid you ten dollars but I've used him all summer so how would five dollars be?' *Bernice C. Hunter, New York*

1975

Last Man In

BY EDWARD STANHAM

We double-figure batsmen (and I refer to batting order, not batting average, which would be presumptuous) have a very different view of those evening games of club cricket from that enjoyed by the demi-gods who bat from one to nine. Still, we are useful, even essential members of the team; we provide the spare umpire, the scorer, the substitute and the transport; we are the music-makers, the movers of screens.

We tend to have an enormous respect for the real cricketers, those large relaxed monolithic men with stark Anglo-Saxon names like Syd Trog, who wear variegated caps and carry long sausage-shaped cricket bags. They seem to have some secret of communication with the genius of cricket which is denied to us, for when taking guard they will make magical symbols in the turf with the end of a bail, or walk half-way down the pitch to tap out morse code signals on the ground with the back of a bat. We on the other hand have simply not got the nerve to take guard and then glare round at each fielder in turn as if cowing him by personality alone and

daring him to stop a fine shot to the boundary. We take guard merely as a formality to indicate to the umpire that we have at last arrived at the right end.

… We try to understand and sometimes even rashly to use the real cricketer's vocabulary; but it is very difficult. To us a 'fine leg' is something which appears below a mini-skirt and 'body-line' is all my eye and Raquel Welch.

However we sometimes actually have to bat and that means unpacking the cricket bag. Mine is made of brown paper and contains but one item of equipment, the batsman's *sine qua non*. I have heard mathematicians refer to it as Q.E.D., *quod erat defendendum*. Then we have to find a bat from the left-overs kindly donated to the club by defunct members. The choice usually rests between the one with the cachet of having HARROW stamped on it – or it would have if it had not lost the portion of wood which carried the H – and the curved and mahogany-coloured one on the back of which is still discernible a faint circle containing what looks like 'specially neglected, Jack Hobbs'. The pads may or may not be a pair and the batting gloves will probably still be gently steaming from the last user.

Finally a wicket falls and it is time to go in and bat. This is the moment when our morale is at its lowest ebb and our legs refuse to function because somehow or other the right pad strap has got done up into the left pad buckle …

On arrival at the crease we are surprised to find one of the fielders standing very close at a sort of silly-point but unaccountably wearing pads. Eventually recognising him as our own Number 10 we hurry down to the opposite end and take guard, once again vowing to stay in long enough to find out whether it is better to wear long-distance glasses and not see the ball or reading glasses and have an invisible bowler.

Rambler at Large

BY CHRISTOPHER HALL

Recovery and loss

On a hot Saturday in July 1963 my newspaper sent me to report a railway propaganda tour organised by a body called SRUBLUK (the Society for the Reinvigoration of Unremunerative Branch Lines in the United Kingdom) – now known by the less comic title of the Railway Invigoration Society.

Dr. Beeching's report, *The Reshaping of British Railways*, had been published a few months before. It seemed that nearly every branch line in the country was threatened – as indeed they nearly all were. SRUBLUK's idea was to travel on as many of the lines threatened in Devon as could be managed in a day trip from Paddington, stopping off to encourage local councillors and defence societies in their resistance to Beeching.

Somewhere south of Newton Poppleford, on what used to be the London and South Western branch to Budleigh Salterton (all gone now), I fell into conversation with the oldest member of the party – a gallant lady aged over 80 from the cathedral city of Wells.

I thought that what she had to say might make a quote for my story and indeed it did, for she produced an analogy at once so bitter-sweetly apposite and yet so far-fetched in its linking of great with minor tragedy that her words stay in my mind long after the piece has been written and the page torn from my notebook.

She said: 'Reading the list of stations to be closed' (she meant the list in the back of the Beeching report) 'was like reading the casualty lists from the front in *The Times* during the First World War. The lists were so long. And just as the war took the best and nicest people you knew, so the closures will take all one's favourite places.'

1976

Cows in Clover

BY D.J. DAVIES

When we sold our Jersey herd in Devon recently after 25 years we were anxious about the future welfare of the animals. They were all home-bred and to us real and individual personalities, almost like part of a large family circle.

Against professional advice we decided to advertise and sell them privately, rather than let an auctioneer auction the stock on the farm. This probably yielded a lower return, but we knew where each animal was going and that it was certain of a good home ...

The most interesting buyers wanted house cows. The dream of self-sufficiency and getting away from it all on a few acres still has appeal; besides, we are in a holiday area and visitors do not feel they have a real farm holiday without cream every day.

One lady phoning said she had two acres of grass knee-high, and wanted a cow to clear it up. Some cow! A second lady needed a cow with the unusual stipulation that it must be dry for the next four months. But there was a good reason: she had

never milked before, and was allowing herself the four months to practise on the dry cow and thus be proficient at milking when the cow calved.

Another lady newly arrived in the country from the Midlands wanted a house cow with the cast-iron guarantee that it was in-calf, but was appalled at the fee the vet might charge for a pregnancy diagnosis. 'I got a test at the chemist's back home for £1.50,' she protested indignantly ...

But the most interesting and delightful of our customers was the titled lady who lived some miles away. She phoned repeatedly asking if we would call and see 'if what she had to offer the cow was adequate', and was so persistent that it seemed churlish not to go.

The farmhouse was down a long lane so badly rutted that we left our car half-way and walked the rest. Fighting our way through the brambles and nettles to her front door we were greeted by the lady herself. She sported an old battered hat of the type used by soldiers in the

Western Desert during the last war, and although it was a hot muggy day was wearing a mac tied with old baler twine and Wellington boots.

'Do come in,' she said. She was a charming lady of some 60 years of age and we took to her at once, but the inside of her house gave us a bit of a shock. In the inglenook fireplace of the old farmhouse kitchen was an unmade bed, the dog-eared army blankets thrown back in disarray, while from the adjoining room on the right came the unmistakable sound of a horse chewing oats. This turned out to be a mare with her foal, happily bedded down in what would probably have been the best room in earlier days.

The lady obviously lived and slept in the old kitchen and shared the room with her two Labradors and five cats. Each cat had its own armchair with its name painted boldly on the chair back. She told us the heat the animals generated kept the house warm in the coldest weather.

'This is where I thought your cow could live,' she told us, opening a door into a room on the left. 'Would she be happy here?'

The cow would certainly have been happy, kept in luxury to which it had never been accustomed. The room opened out on to a vegetable garden that had been allowed to run to seed, with a paddock beyond. But cows are animals which make a lot of sloppy mess. The feeding, watering, and above all the inevitable mucking-out would have been intolerable under such conditions, and she was gently persuaded against the idea.

Wild Life and Tame

WELL HELD, SIR!

Threading my way through a throng of people in the heart of my native city, I saw a dark object suddenly appear over my head: instantly my two hands reached up and snatched a terrified town pigeon down to waist level as I side-stepped an oncoming pedestrian. Thirteen years of goalkeeping in amateur soccer had doubtlessly set up this somewhat embarrassing reaction. My last glimpse of the feathered 'football' was as it skilfully darted away among a maze of human feet.

Fred Keating, Cheshire

1977

Peg-Leg Percy

At the end of one lambing season a lamb was born with its back leg missing from the elbow joint. I decided to leave him until twins were born, when I would kill off the deformed lamb and foster one twin on to his mother. Three days went by. The invalid was still alive enjoying the spring sunshine: he deserved to live. Carving an artificial leg out of wood I fastened it to the lamb's stump. As he grew so I made him larger legs. He had no special treatment as he ran with the rest of the flock. Being a male the day came when he was fat enough to send to the fat-stock market. On arriving at the weigh-bridge the Ministry grader told me he would be classed as a casualty and no subsidy was payable on him. He was reprieved a little longer for I brought him home and turned him back out with his mother. Time went by and the subsidy was reduced to nil. It was time for Percy to go. Loading him up in the truck our eyes met; he seemed to sense what was in store for him. How could I eat lamb for next Sunday's dinner? I weakened and led him to the large lawn that surrounds my house. Percy is still there, saving me all that sweating labour of mowing it.

Sydney W. Handy, Worcestershire

Heads Down

My grandfather's farmer employer once asked him to plant a dozen blackcurrant bushes. When he had done so, my grandfather was told, 'That's not the way – you plant them with the roots uppermost!' My grandfather thought the man was joking at first, but no, he insisted that it should be done like that. Anyway, during the winter the aerial roots were cut back and next spring a profusion of young stems arose from the branches which should have been above ground from the start but had now begun as subterranean suckers. There was of course no fruit that year, but the following summer produced a bumper crop – the finest my grandfather had ever seen.

It seems there was certain method in the farmer's madness for blackcurrants fruit from young wood, whereas redcurrants fruit from the old.

Anthony Wootton, Buckinghamshire

COUNTRYMAN CLUB

HAVE FAITH

We are told that there is no cure for the Dutch elm disease that has caused so many of these trees to be destroyed. However, as I have been practising faith healing for a number of years, it struck me that trees could be cured, too. Through the kindness of the Director of Parks in Cardiff, six afflicted elm trees were saved for me, from those due to be cut down in September 1975. The 1976 report from the Director says that all six of those trees have been cured of the disease. All were about eighty years old and had been diseased for some years; this appears to be the first time that Dutch elm disease has been cured this way. If any reader is interested in this method and would write to me, I will be very pleased to help.

Dewi Turton, 90 Cathedral Road, Cardiff

In the summer of 1978 Jane Grigson's article describing 'The cook's dream garden' was pictured exactly as she described, complete with caves for sheltering citrus plants in winter, forcing chicory, growing mushrooms, farming snails, storing produce, drying vegetables, and pressing grapes from the vineyard above.

1978-1989

Urban Migrants

A nother change of editor in 1981 heralded a big change of attitude and content in *The Countryman* and perhaps it began to lose its way a little. Christopher Hall, who took over the editorship from Crispin Gill in the summer of 1981, had been chairman of the Ramblers' Association and the emphasis changed from the country dweller to the country visitor, especially those on foot. As Crispin Gill said in 1978, concerning the new chairman of the Countryside Commission, Lord Winstanley, but applicable more widely to *Countryman* readers: 'He looks like the urban man who seeks his recreation in the countryside, which makes him representative of the majority of country-goers today.'

Colour photographs were used on the cover for the first time in 1981, and the price of the journal began to rise alarmingly. It was 55p at the end of 1978; it broke the £1 barrier in 1983 and hit £1.50 in 1989.

This was a period of second homes, city farmers, bypasses, airports, acronyms, early recycling, 'caring for the countryside', 'amenity' values, 'horticulture', food surpluses throughout the western world, tentative steps into organic farming, a proliferation of advisory services and assorted acronyms, an increasingly vociferous anti-blood sports movement and, of course, Margaret Thatcher who, like many a new prime minister before her, accepted the invitation to write an article in *The Countryman* in 1980. It was the period in which the urban country-goer triumphed over the true country dweller, and the pages of the review showed an increasingly strong anti-farmer element. The tone became angry, and perhaps a little shrill.

To those of us who did and do live in the country, it seems quite extraordinary that the 'hurricane' of October 1987, which wreaked such havoc in parts of the landscape, tore down a massive and unprecedented number of trees and brought many people to tears, was barely mentioned in *The Countryman*.

1978

How 'The Outsider' Came In – to Cornwall

BY COLIN WILSON

It has often struck me that the townsman, on his occasional visits to the country, gets far more out of it than the man who was born there. I have lived in the country for more than twenty years now – in a little Cornish fishing village near Mevagissey – and I know many born countrymen who swear they would feel suffocated to death in a city. Yet I doubt whether many of them feel that electrical tingle of sheer freedom that I often get when I draw the bedroom curtains in the morning and look out at the cliffs and the sea.

That, of course, is because I was born in a large city – Leicester. Moreover, the major event of my childhood was the war, which seemed to go on forever … The countryside was somewhere marvellous and remote, that you read about in Jeffrey Farnol, or (later), in Richard Jefferies and W.H. Hudson …

It was not until I was 14, and my grandfather presented me with a second-hand bicycle, that I finally had a chance to explore the countryside I had read about so much. And, to be honest, it was not quite the revelation I had expected. It is true that there was often a marvellous sensation of freedom as I set out for Warwick or Matlock on a sunny morning, but this would evaporate after an hour or so, and then there was just the sensation of pedalling along a main road, keeping close to the grass verge to avoid the cars that came roaring past …

Perhaps I love the country so much because my ancestors were countrymen – a hypothesis I shall never be able to verify, since my grandfathers on both sides were foundlings. But I suspect that the real reason is that everyone has this same deep need, to belong to a certain place, to feel a part of it, to watch its seasons changing and to know all its landmarks. Not all 'outsiders' are social misfits or metaphysical rebels. Some of them only want to get back to a place where they can actually hear the wind and watch the leaves change colour.

Wild Life and Tame

EMERGENCY CALLS

In my irresponsible youth I ... discovered that three loud whistles would send flocks of sheep frantic and charging across the field like the Light Brigade. When I became a goods train guard and was taking a train from Alsager to Crewe, I saw a huge flock of sheep in a field, all nicely rounded up, complete with shepherd and dogs. Unable to resist the temptation, I gave three loud whistles and instantly the whole flock spread out in all directions, while the shepherd danced about, shaking his fists. I thought it highly amusing at the time, but later realised what a despicable trick it was and from that day to this have not repeated the experiment. Norman W. Venables, Cheshire

Scent Home

The nurse was making her visit to a school in Ireland and sent home one boy, who was in a filthy condition, with a note asking that he be washed before coming to school. His mother sent the following reply:

'Dear Miss the Nurse – You sent wee Harry home from school becas he smelds. He smelds just like his Da and I have lived with him for 20 years. What is good enough for me is good enough for you. I suppose you are some auld maid who doesnt know the smell of a good man anyhow. P.S. Wee Harry wasnt sent to school to be smelt, he is not a rose, he was sent to school to be teched.'

D.O.F. Lumsden, Warminster, Wilts

Calling Down Nightjars

BY JEREMY BENNETT

There is much about nightjars that is unique among British birds. They are mysterious, emerging when most other birds have gone to their roost; they are elusive, wise-looking and sound like nothing else on earth. … I had never seen this strange bird until I visited a bracken-clad hillside in North Somerset last summer.

It was typical nightjar country: a gentle slope where the debris of felled conifers snuggled in thick heather and green bracken fronds … It was nine o'clock on the evening of the sixth of July … At ten o'clock a cool breeze made me fidget and pull my collar up. It was almost too dark to see …

I rose to my feet and walked about to restore the circulation in my legs, and then I heard it: a gentle, yet insistent churring, that could only be a nightjar, somewhere in the bracken below the path. Another started up in the distance, and then another, quite close, until the night, which had been dead and silent, became alive with one of the weirdest sounds in nature. The air seemed to vibrate with the undulating tone, and then, after a crescendo of sound, the churring stopped, and the silence returned, even heavier than before.

'*Koo-ek! koo-ek!*' This was the hunting call, which the nightjars use to keep in contact with one another; they would now be jinking through the heather, snapping up moths with their huge, gaping mouths.

I moved into the spruce grove, and immediately the churring started again, directly above my head. I looked up to see my first nightjar, perching … on a dead branch, its throat vibrating rapidly as it produced its marvellous sound. This was a moment for some serious research – I had read that the variation in the tone of a nightjar's churring occurs when the bird turns its head from side to side, but this particular individual continued for over ten minutes without a pause, and did not turn its head more than once, although the pitch of the churring changed six times. I had a perfect view of his slender, hawklike form, and could have touched him with a broom handle from where I stood.

Finally, the churring ran down into a low chuckling sound as the nightjar took off, clapped his wings over his back with a very audible crack, and soared away over the bracken. As it flew, it called '*koo-ek*' three times, and on an impulse, I called a reply. It was a poor imitation, but it had the desired effect.

As I stepped from the cover of the trees, the nightjar turned, flew towards me, and hovered over my head like a fairy kestrel, so close that I could feel the draught of its wingbeats, and see its huge, round eyes. Did it, I wondered, think that I was another male nightjar intruding upon its territory, or was it merely living up to its reputation of being an intensely curious species?

For several magic seconds, we faced each other, and then, as I walked away, still imitating its call, it followed, obviously fascinated and unsure of what to make of me. Another male appeared, flashing its white tail and wing spots, and flew low over the ground in front of me. He vanished for a few seconds, and then reappeared followed by two females, and the whole party proceeded to circle about my head, calling frantically. I felt like a nocturnal pied piper as the four birds followed me for 20 yards along the path.

By way of experiment, I next lay on my back in the heather, and clapped my hands several times. The two females instantly departed, but the inquisitive males hovered close to my face, clapping their wings whenever I clapped my hands …

Eventually, after about ten minutes of this memorable encounter, I decided out of pity for the mystified nightjars, to get up and leave them to their hunting. The sight of a man suddenly rising from the ground is normally enough to send a bird screaming to safety, but not these. They merely increased altitude slightly, and continued to stick close to me. Occasionally, one would fly off in pursuit of a moth, enabling me to admire its fast, dashing flight and agile twisting as if homing in on its whirring prey, but then it would return, hovering and standing on its tail over the bracken before joining its companion above my head. I walked on with my two nightjars into the taller trees and the gradual descent that would take me back to the road and my waiting car. Then, on long pointed wings, they banked sharply to the right, and were gone into the darkness.

" Producing a merganser from his bag after a wildfowling expedition on the Dovey Estuary, my neighbour was hesitant about its eating qualities. 'Tell you what to do with him,' said an onlooker, 'put him in a dish along with a firebrick. Cover them both up with a big slice of bacon fat, then cook in a hot oven for three hours. Remove them from the oven, throw away the bird and eat the brick.' " Jack Jennings, Hereford

As a Farmer Sees It

by Hew Watt

As a boy taking my annual train journey north from London for summer holidays, I did not need mile-posts to judge how far we had gone. First, black-and-white Friesian cows predominated, providing London's daily milk supply, but as we sped north on the east coast route, it was not long before brown-and-white Dairy Shorthorns took over, supplying both beef and milk, and then ruby red Lincolns fattened in yards and providing manure for arable farming.

Further north, Dairy Shorthorns changed to blockier animals on the uplands plus blue-grey cows suckling their calves, showing that Scotland with its black Angus and Galloway cattle was not far away. Dairy herds by this time had changed to brown-and-white Ayrshires with Viking horns, coping with harder weather better than our soft cows of the south! In Scotland the Ayrshire predominated for milk with Aberdeen Angus for beef, plus the attractive ragged Highland cattle that survive in the cold north.

If I travelled the western route I saw more Jersey and Guernsey cows plus Hereford beef cattle with their rich ruby coats and white faces. All these breeds originated to suit soil, climate and economic needs of local farming communities; and with travel limited to horse or rail only crossing bulls went far beyond their counties of origin. Today all this has changed; intensification of livestock production into much larger herds, followed by cost-effective advice from advisory services, means that practically all dairy herds are black-and-white, crossed in some cases with Hereford and Angus for beef.

Artificial insemination gives a wide choice, hence continental breeds of Charolais, Limousin and Simmental are fast bringing new landscapes of creams, duns and sandy mixtures across our meadows. Just as your car or TV set often has a foreign name, so the beef on your plate often has an input from an exotic French gentleman. Unfortunately he usually arrives by test-tube.

1979

No Through Road

BY BARRY COOPER (local government transport adviser)

… There will always be roads, such as motorways and 'A' roads, that serve wider areas than those through which they pass … But most people do not want the remaining roads to be for anything more than local use; they do not want through-traffic to be encouraged on to them. Yet, if more money is made available, and local roads continue to be improved and kept in good condition, they will become easier to use and so more motorists will use them as through-routes … One alternative to the gradual improvement of country roads to consistent standards would be for county councils to delegate all decision-making on local roads to local people. Each parish council could be given the job of deciding spending priorities in its area, within an annual lump-sum, and be accountable for the results.

> *Animals, like people, have a pecking order but the choice of boss still surprises me. While admiring Tom Brewis's group of fully grown Aberdeen Angus bulls grazing peacefully at Kelso, I was struck by the presence of a jack donkey. 'What's he doing there?' I asked. 'Stops the bulls fighting', Tom replied. 'He's definitely the Governor!'* Hew Watt

1980

Confessions of a Farm Biologist

BY B. REILLY

… There was a story current in 1930 about one adviser who travelled by train one very hot summer's afternoon from Edinburgh to Perth and, from there, a long way by country bus up one of the glens. He arrived at last at a lonely little school where a group of farmers had gathered to hear his talk. He spoke at length about the dangers of dirty milk, of the bacteria that accompanied the dirt and how they came to be in the milk. Words like Mastitis, Tuberculosis, Coli, Aerogenes and Streptococcus bespattered his audience as he stressed the importance of washing udders and the rear of the cow before milking. He laboured nobly and was rewarded by a leafy rustle of hand-clapping. The chairman thanked him and called for comments. Fifteen silent seconds passed before a stringy Calvinist arose from the back seats. 'Well, Mr. Chairman,' he said, 'we dae thank Mr. Smith for gie'n us his crack aboot his coos in E'nbra', but I say if God had intended us tae hae cleaner milk, he would hae put the udders at the ither end o' the coo.'

Old Cheshire countrywoman, coming up the garden path: 'Ay, I'm coming, slow and steady, like a donkey's gallop.'

Henpecked Ulster husband, telling a friend what his wife had given him for tea the previous evening: 'Hot tongue an' cold shoulder.'

Shock Treatment

A young member of a gang of woodmen in the Forest of Dean, suffering from agonising toothache, was told by a timber haulier driving a tractor that a mild electric shock would jolt the nerve and effect an immediate cure. The haulier offered his services as medicine man, explaining that for the price of a pint of cider he would administer the shock treatment by simply touching the tooth with a thin length of wire to the twelve-volt battery on the tractor. The youth was in such pain that he would have tried anything once; he accepted the offer. The haulier produced a length of flex from his tool box and told his victim to hold the bare end of the wire against the decayed molar, stand quite still and look the other way. Then while we watched the quack doctor attached the other end of the wire to a sparking plug on the tractor and with no further warning started the engine. As it sprang into life the youth sprang into the air with a cry, then while his colleagues laughed hilariously, stood still with a look of amazement, and after a pause declared with a smile of relief that the pain had vanished. He paid his torturer the agreed fee without another word. The haulier told me afterwards that he himself, while suffering toothache, had accidentally touched the plug of a running tractor and noticed that from that moment the toothache ceased …

One day in 1941 we were extracting pit wood across a steep ravine by running the props on a ¾-in wire rope to a hard road on the other side of the valley, some 200 yards distant. The rope was fixed firmly to large trees on either side of the ravine. As I sat on my own by the top end of the rope it began to vibrate, eventually increasing until the movement was in inches, setting up a deep humming sound. I was greatly puzzled until I saw a Queen Bee target towing plane flying out across the sea from the artillery range at Towyn, a few miles from where we were working on a hill in Cardiganshire. I then realised that the engine drone and consequent vibrations were in sympathy with our wire rope which was behaving like the string on a musical instrument.

Jack Jennings, Hereford

" *Notice outside a farm in Gloucestershire: 'Wanted – Woman to wash, iron and milk three cows'.* "

'We Cannot Take the Countryside for Granted ...'

THE PRIME MINISTER [MARGARET THATCHER]

Anyone who cares for the countryside – its economic prosperity and its social well-being as well as its physical appearance – also has a special affection for *The Countryman*. For more than half a century, it has voiced that concern and established for itself a firm reputation as a journal of profound good sense and one which brings to its readers, both in town and countryside, the authentic flavour of rural life.

Lately there has been increased unease about the future of our rural areas. A new term, 'rural deprivation', has been coined to describe those problems which lead some to fear wholesale decline of village communities. A series of publications have drawn attention to them, notably reports from the Associations of County and District Councils, and from the National Council of Social Service. I recognise the fears expressed and the importance of ensuring that the needs and aspirations of those who live and work in our villages are not overlooked. We intend to do all we can, including a new, flexible approach to planning, to help conserve the

countryside and to promote not only its traditional industries – agriculture, forestry and food processing – but also small businesses which can play a key role in generating new jobs.

I know, of course, of the particular concerns about the closure of village schools. Small village schools have had a long and honourable history, contributing greatly to the welfare and traditions of the area whose children they have educated. And I am acutely conscious of the loss of cultural and social activities that can be created by their closure. All these factors are considered most carefully, along with the education arguments, before approval is given to close a school. As many such schools have closed over the last four decades there may be little further scope for 'rationalisation' in this way. I therefore expect the majority of future proposals to relate to schools in towns.

Adequate public transport is essential in rural areas. Although many country people own cars, many others depend on public transport for getting about. We want to see new types of service develop in the countryside to supplement existing buses and we want to encourage greater efficiency to keep the costs down. Our proposals for reforming bus licensing will make it easier for people to start up new bus services and to help each other by sharing cars and other small vehicles: this will do much to help country people make essential journeys.

On conservation, too, we have already taken steps. We are now working on legislation on countryside and wild life which will secure important advances in protection of birds, key habitats and landscape, including the conservation of moorland. An important feature will be the power proposed for local authorities to make management agreements for the purpose of protecting land of scenic importance.

In addition, we are legislating to provide for the formation of the National Heritage Fund. Independent trustees will be able to assist in the purchase not only of heritage buildings and works of art but also of land – of scenic, scientific or historic significance – of such outstanding quality that it merits holding in trust for the nation's benefit. Furthermore, we propose to retain the system whereby land, art and buildings can be accepted by the government in lieu of payment of Capital Transfer Tax.

We cannot take the countryside for granted. We shall show, as a Government, that that is a lesson we have learned well.

[Editor's note: This article was accompanied by photographs of Mrs. Thatcher, perfectly coiffed, dressed in a smart cape and carrying a horn handled walking-stick, standing in a muddy farmyard and offering a tentative handful of straw to bemused and wary cattle. V.L.P]

1981

Horsing About in the Forest

BY ALAN COREN

Dawn the colour of a herring's belly, and the chill February fog thick on the New Forest, trees and cottage roofs rising above it like the casualties of some dam-doomed valley waiting in sullen resignation for the final obliterating flood.

A good day for assassinations.

I came out of Court Copse at a circumspect canter, swept the wet light with slitted eyes, and took off, fast, across Furzley Common, after Sir Walter Tyrrell. I could see his vanishing haunches, just; perhaps half a mile off, and he was galloping hard, but I had right on my side, and right is worth a few furlongs any day of the week.

He had, after all, just let go an arrow that had snapped the monarch's sternum like a dead twig, filled his lungs with blood, and left the uncertain English throne in even greater chaos than it had enjoyed at breakfast. I hold no great brief for William Rufus, never did, but God put him there, and men of honour accept God's embassy.

If it *was* Tyrrell up ahead. The way

fog shrouds the Forest sometimes, moves trees about, makes heaths of copses, turns shrubs to wolves and shuffles dwellings, the rider can be sure of nothing.

I chased the horse for a couple of miles, through Bramshaw Wood and Nomansland, out across Hamptworth Common, up Cloven Hill and past Loosehanger Copse; I lost it between Bohemia and Lover. It is worth losing something, if you are able to say you lost it between Bohemia and Lover.

Not that it mattered, anyhow. Face it, friends, Tyrrell has been dead nine hundred years. What I had lost was a forest cob, shag-coated for winter, but fast and clever, galloping through the chest-high mist, legless as a rubber bathing-horse. I reined my own horse in; we stood steaming in our private fog; I lit a cigarette, compounding the varieties of swirl. It was the only anachronism, that orange speck: when the Bastard's auburn son popped his royal clogs that day, there was nothing for his distraught aides to pass around and light, while they wondered what the hell to do next. Six centuries would have to roll before Hawkins brought lung cancer back from the New World.

The New Forest is the best place there is to pursue historical fantasy: especially on horseback. A horse entitles you to dream: it is a time capsule. Those who are minded to fantasise in cars can go back only a decade or two, take the North Circular in their Cortinas and chase Nuvolari's Alfa through the suburban chicanes (and doubtless wipe themselves out, reality being what it is, against the flank of some incautious juggernaut); you cannot fantasise aright on some sleek glass-fibre-hulled catamaran (Drake had no sonar), or shoot down Richthofen from your Concorde seat. But horses have not changed: mount up, ride into the middle of these uncultivated hundred thousand acres, beneath the shade of eighteenth-century oaks, and no one can deny your right to lose yourself in English history.

Even if you have spent the bulk of your life as an urban yokel. Until I was 35, I looked upon the horse as nothing more than something to watch out for in French casseroles. In my childhood, it is true, I knew the horse gave milk, left eggs, and improved roses; but after United Dairies electrified their floats, the horse and I parted company for a quarter of a century, except for those fleeting contretemps when second favourites loped off with my rent-money. But six years ago, with my life on the cusp, 35 down and 35, with average luck, to go, it was borne in upon me that weekends should have more to offer than a toxic oblivion compounded of Jimmy Hill and Vat 69, spent huddled behind the treble-glazing to keep out the worst of the metropolitan blight; and I went rural …

My Country

BY SPIKE MILLIGAN

I love the British countryside, though my access to it came late, thanks to Adolf Hitler. Let me explain. I was born one torrid afternoon in 1918 at the Cantonment Military Hospital of a British remount depot in Ahmednagar, India, and my early years were spent in the junglesque atmosphere of a Kipling boyhood. My father was never stationed in any giant metropolis like Bombay, Karachi or Calcutta – but in places like Poona and Belgaum, all semi-rural. Being born to the Regiment (the Royal Horse Artillery), I was riding through the open Indian countryside at the tender age of four. I existed for the out-of-doors; to me, houses were for changing your clothes in, so my boyhood was spent in wild countryside with trees like the tamarind, the mango, the phorum. Farmers used wooden ploughs and they planted by hand with a piece of sharpened 'luckery' stick. To me, all cattle were emaciated, and the ringing of goat bells ran through my boyhood; instead of foxes and badgers, it was monkeys, mongooses, cobras and scorpions. The sun blazed on the parched maidans in summer; they steamed as the monsoon rains deluged the landscape. All this ...

So, imagine the explosive effect at the age of 21, of seeing the lush of the English countryside for the first time. It was an experience that bordered on the hallucinogenic. From India I came to live in the black, fog-bound gloom of London in the depressing 1930s. Then came 'the call to arms' and one golden sunlit day in June 1940 I caught the 9.10 train from Victoria to report to the regiment at Bexhill-on-Sea. Imagine the privilege of living in an English seaside country town with most of the residents fled, and *no tourists*. The first thing was the air: that attar-like perfume of ozone and chlorophyll was a heady mixture. Unused to its scent, I kept asking people if there was a perfume factory nearby.

What opened up the countryside were the route marches. Marching down a hedgerow-lined country lane to me was an experience that I presume pot-smokers must have. For a start I had never seen hedgerow flowers. At every halt ('Fall out for a smoke') I was aware of curious khaki eyes watching Gunner Milligan observing these small wayside miracles. I've no idea what it is in a wayside flower that makes a human being its slave ...

Hard-hit Sussex farmers (whose workers were sitting in trenches in

Libya) called on us for help. Standing on one of those magnificent Sussex farm wagons (now almost extinct) with a pitchfork, baling hay, I felt like God. I had become so emotionally integrated with the country that even the farm implements were exciting. I wondered at the elegance of those two slender curving steel horns of the hay-fork; not only its aesthetic quality but that it was the perfect tool for the job.

… Then English cattle, dripping with beef and awash with milk; were these the same species as those wretched Indian skeletons? What a sight on a sunlit day to stand on a high point of the Downs and watch a landscape of alarming green, dotted with the red-and-white of the Herefords, the black-and-white of the Friesians and dun of the Jerseys.

This was the English countryside – it sang to you – this was the reason Constable never wanted to paint anything else … That was then. Now, 41 years later, alas, our countryside (and I stress *our* countryside) is being eroded and mutilated. Cruel farming methods are being evolved.

… 'Prairie' farming is to blame, and factory farming is another villain.

Farmers did not dream up intensive farming. No, it was the pressure of greater demand at cheaper prices, so that families, to whom chicken was a luxury, could have one whenever they wanted. Factory Farmer Giles is only obeying the demand for more and cheaper food.

… What is killing the countryside is pressure from increasing population and affluence; depression or no, people still have more money than of yore, and there are more of us than of yore. The result is tremendous pressure on land and the fruits of the land. The only way to reverse this physical and moral erosion is first to stabilise our numbers and then in controlled and humane fashion *reduce* them.

… If we are to save our delightful countryside – there is only one way. Malthus was right: if you want the countryside to survive – small families please, preferably vegetarians.

1982

The Rape of the Hill

BY HARRY HARGREAVES

Across the valley from my window is a Somerset hill which fills the western skyline completely. Creech Hill, from a Celtic word *cryc* meaning hill, is still farming land, with Friesians dotting its slopes like black-and-white greenfly. Just below its surface of thin topsoil and stone brash, it has an armour-plating of solidified sea bed, millions of years old, rock-hard and fossil-filled.

… This halcyon, rural scene – complete with a farmer who looked like Father Time's twin and stumped along the hedgerows with his passive cattle on the way down to milk them (himself and by hand), a poacher popping ferrets into rabbit holes, badger-watching boys from the school, a horse-rider or two, buzzards and hawks circling and calling, foxes by day and by night – until some five years ago seemed settled and gently right for the hill, despite the spreading battery-hen farm near its crown.

Today it also has a well-established maggot farm and a well-established protest group objecting to the appalling stench. Its slopes have great grassless circuits torn to tortuous shapes by hundreds of scramble motor-bikes. They fume and scream endlessly up and around in highly-organised contests, which also fill the upper pastures with hundreds of parked vehicles and drown the area in noise from a powerful public-address system.

Its remaining topknot of trees covers a pheasant chick-rearing venture; and clay pigeon shoots, grass-skiing, and fox- and badger-hunting in a pick-up with a red searchlight roaring up and down the fields at midnight, celebrate the great leap forward into the late twentieth century of the hill. Army helicopters and light aircraft often land on it and service aircraft of all kinds fly low around it using it as a pylon. One buzzard was still to be seen up to last summer but, like the regular patrolling kestrel and mate, not since.

Designated for the conservation of its beauty many years ago, the only protection that the hill seems to have is its armour-plating below the stone brash; but if fossil-hunters get into that, I could well have a levelled site to gaze out over, into the far distance, for miles.

Regional billhook designs from a 1982 article by Jack Wilson.

"*'We're getting to the stage where the only animal on the farm with room to turn will be the accountant's Jaguar. We're denying the species that have served us so well the rights and dignity due to them.'*" Dr Alan Long, Research Adviser to the Vegetarian Society, speaking on rights for animals in March this year

Down on the Farm

BY HUMPHREY PHELPS

HUSBANDRY OR HIGH TECHNOLOGY?

… The substitution of urban economics for the older rural economics, the insistence upon output per man and cheap food has, quite logically, led to agribusiness at the expense of husbandry. Traditional farming, which was no enemy to conservation, has been replaced by factory farming, poisonous sprays, the destruction of the countryside and its wildlife. The de-humanising of farming has smashed the old rural structure which took generations to build.

In my district, agribusiness in its more overt forms has not yet arrived; this countryside between the Severn and the Forest of Dean by its very nature does not lend itself to large-scale arable farming. Here we still have family farms, trees and hedgerows. But in the last 20 years at least a score of small farms have been absorbed into larger holdings in my immediate neighbourhood. Orchards have been grubbed out and every year a few hedges are removed. Some farmers have received large sums of money to quit milk production; others have had large sums to increase milk production. The traditional mixed husbandry has been replaced by specialisation; the old values scorned. Mechanisation has meant the land provides little work for local people either directly or indirectly; farming looks to the town for its needs and our country people have had to look to the town for their livelihoods. We may have a noisier countryside, but we do not have a busier one.

… I do not share the general view among farmers that they can do what they like because they are producing food for the nation, forgetting that they are producing food as a means of livelihood. I do not like paying taxes, but I see no reason for buying machinery I neither need nor can afford. But so many farmers have to have the latest machines or equipment just as a child yearns for a new toy, and which are, like the toy, soon abandoned … At present it is computers for cows, which cost thousands of pounds. When I feel I must have a computer it will be time I gave up farming. I think, perhaps, it is time I put up a notice: £1 TO SEE THE OLD-FASHIONED FARMER. We are getting rare and besides I could do with the money.

Wild Life and Tame

CUBSTITUTE

Terrified by the noise of our metal dustbins being emptied, our miniature long-haired dachshund bolted one morning into the busy street. After a fruitless search, we were informed in the evening by the local police station that she had been found. Who had found her? She had been turned in by a friendly fox, the duty sergeant told us, the significance of the remark not penetrating until we called on the lady who reported the find. Looking out of a bedroom window, she saw a fox in her garden, not unusual because the garden backed on a railway cutting; but this fox had in its mouth a cub, which it set down in the centre of the lawn, then slunk away into the shrubbery to watch it. After a few minutes the little animal got to its feet and edged nervously towards the house, whereupon the fox dashed out, picked it up by the scruff of the neck and put it back in the centre of the garden. Only then did the lady realise that the 'cub' was in fact a small dog. She rushed out to rescue it and the fox disappeared over the back garden fence. F.M. Bunbury, West Midlands

1984

The Legend of Enklefield

BY RICHARD JERRED

Two young heads were passing below the garden wall that morning when I heard a voice exclaim, 'They'm combining Enklefield today, I see!'

Enklefield? Where on earth was Enklefield? They turned when I called, 'Hey! Where's Enklefield?'

Disbelief showed in the elder boy's face and I had to repeat the question. 'There!' he said simply, pointing across the valley to where a red combine harvester was relentlessly devouring a field of wheat and casting out the golden spoil.

'But that's Quarter-Mile field,' I protested …

It had always been Quarter-Mile field. Hadn't I known the man who had farmed it and, in the 1930s, walked beside him as he broke its surface with a horse-drawn plough? Wasn't this the long, narrow field that early in World War II sprouted an unusual crop? Stout wooden poles were planted, to frustrate invading German glider pilots and bring about, we hoped, the demise of their unwelcome passengers. Then the truth

struck me. *I had once been present at the making of field history.*

In April 1941, my leave, preparatory to joining a bomber squadron, was drawing to a close; along with most other residents of the village, I wondered would they come again tonight? As the daylight faded, the sky over the city some 20 miles away reflected the unextinguished fires of the previous night's raid, turned to a blood-red. Then came the throb of unsynchronised engines and the distant red turned first to yellow and finally to ochre.

By dawn the sky was silent again and the glow had faded into a black pall which denoted burning oil. How seriously had they damaged the vital naval base? It was then that the infallible grape-vine that operates in all villages reported an enemy bomber downed in the nearby fields. Determined to see first-hand, if not my enemy, the equipment he used, I set off on a borrowed bicycle.

Several people were standing at the gate, where in front of the aircraft a single, steel-helmeted sentry stood, respirator and gas cape slung in the approved manner and long bayonet attached to the rifle hanging from his shoulder. As I unlatched the gate, for it would have been undignified to have climbed it, he stiffened and pinched out the Woodbine he'd been surreptitiously holding behind his back. He eyed my RAF uniform with suspicion.

'It's all right, sentry! I just want to make sure it's safe before our chaps come and collect it.' He relaxed and I gave him a cigarette to replace his ruined Woodbine, suggesting he didn't smoke it too near the aeroplane. I learned that the crew were already in custody.

In its wheels-up landing, the bomber had ploughed a furrow in the green turf almost as straight as those of my farmer friend, though much, much wider. Somehow, belly on the ground, it was devoid of aggression, assuming instead an air of pathos like an exhausted basset-hound, ears spread on a green hearthrug. The muzzle of the single gun in the transparent nose drooped earthwards while that in the rear-gunner's cupola pointed aimlessly at the empty sky. Inside, amid all the evidence of a hasty exit, it even smelt different from our aircraft. Not wishing to incur the displeasure of authority I didn't stay long, though my inspection was enough to convince me that the Heinkel 111 was decidedly inferior to our own twin-engined bombers.

And that's how Quarter-Mile field came by its new name. If it only takes a little over 40 years for 'The Heinkel Field' to become 'Enklefield', what chance do I have of decoding the names of fields older than the Norman church that stands on the hill overlooking the village?

Are You Walking Comfortably?

by John Hillaby

John Hillaby, now 67, has walked the equivalent of more than four times round the world. He is well equipped to give some guidance even to the casual hiker on how to keep walking feet warm, dry and happy.

… One of my earliest long-distance walks, a transalpine affair, taught me that there are distinct advantages in being able to mingle both among owners of Mercedes and humble folk in mountain villages without looking outlandish. And for me, an information-seeker, a pipe is useful too. I like to think it gives me an air of self-sufficiency. I suppose a man on his own can look wholly at ease, puffing away at a cigarette, but offhand I can't recall seeing one.

… A few wrinkles about wrinkles. 'Arrange' your toes, carefully, before putting on your socks. Little toes in particular are much given to playing piggy-back with their fellows, which is very productive of inter-toe blisters. You will, of course, have cut your toe-nails with care. Pull on your socks slowly and lace up your boots or shoes tightly, but not too tightly. Walking should be an entirely pleasurable exercise. Stop the moment you feel the slightest discomfort. Something chafing? Something too tight? Something intruding? A pin-head-sized piece of grit can become a pea-sized blister in an hour and a limp-provoker in a day's walk. *Never* try to harden your feet by artificial means. Grease or oil them as Olympic long-distance runners do. Olive oil is ideal. And never wear nylon next to your feet.

Wild Life and Tame

A Shock at Dusk

As I walked along a path one evening, a sudden loud, explosive noise under my feet made me jump. I thought I had trodden on one of those party squeakers, made partly of curled paper, that shoot straight when blown, letting out a loud, ugly, wobbly noise. I wondered how it could have got there and looked down. Horrified, I saw that I had trodden on a toad. It was absolutely flat and looked quite dead. As I stared at what I had done, I noticed one of the toad's flattened-out back legs moving slightly. Then it was slowly drawn up to its natural position. One by one the other legs were drawn up too. At the same time its body was gradually filling out again until it was a normal toad once more. I then realised that the noise I had heard was of the air being suddenly expelled from its body and I was very relieved to see it crawl away, apparently none the worse.

Barbara Pauling, East Sussex

Solent Swimmer

About 8am on 18 May this year, with a clear sky and visibility four miles with haze, I was on pilot duties close to the Hamble Point buoy and saw what at first I thought was a piece of branched driftwood, but with a difference: it appeared to be moving quite swiftly. Through binoculars I saw that it was a young roe-buck, swimming towards the shore of Hook Park. I decided to take photographs showing recognisable reference points, but it proved quite awkward, trying to manoeuvre a pilot launch, with the best part of 400hp of diesel engines roaring, close enough, without causing the swimmer undue distress and veering him off his original course. A slight change in direction could have brought him ashore farther north amongst the refinery systems of Fawley or Hamble. I was unable to wait and observe him complete his crossing, but he was swimming strongly and would have had no trouble in reaching the shingle of Hook Park. Trying to retrace his journey and taking a flood-tide into account, I estimate that the buck entered the water somewhere close south-west of Calshot. He had probably swum, with tidal assistance, somewhere in the region of three miles; his reason for taking to the water is open to conjecture. No one, including numerous pilots of long experience (I have plied the Solent/I.o.W. waters for ten years myself) whom I have asked, has ever made a comparable observation. T.E. Dubicki, Isle of Wight

When a Village Is Not a Village

BY H.F. ELLIS

'I got it,' you may hear people say, 'from a shop in the village.'

This is, to my mind, almost a contradiction in terms – as will readily be seen if you contrast it with the unexceptionable 'I got it from the village shop'. A multiplicity of shops, I make bold to say, is the very negation of villagedom, and to talk of *a* shop in the village, rather than, say, 'Mrs. Beale's' or just 'the butcher's', instantly reveals that the speaker has deluded himself into a belief that he lives in a village when he doesn't.

… If you actually live in a village, no question about it arises. If you like to think you live in a village, you don't.

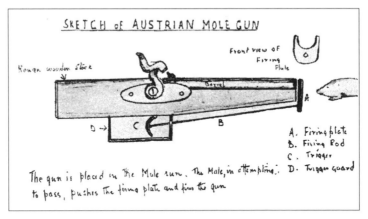

An Austrian gunsmith developed a gun with which unfortunate moles shot themselves by bumping into the firing plate when the muzzle was placed in their runs. This type of gun was still used occasionally by older men in Britain between the wars. It is not clear whether the moles also automatically reloaded the weapon!

1986

Point of No Return

It had been a difficult labour, but it seemed as if the little calf would be born alive after all. The men had had a rope around its legs and were pulling gently to assist the cow's contractions. When the five-year-old girl appeared in the barn, the men looked at her in dismay. Should they hurry her away so that she wouldn't see? There was no time. The cow gave a final heave, the men pulled on the rope, and a steaming little bull-calf dropped on to the straw. The girl pushed her way through the men's legs and, putting her arms around the newborn calf, said, 'You naughty thing! Don't you *ever* get in there again!'

Jana French, Windlesham, Surrey

Englishmen's Knees

BY IRENE RAWNSLEY

Hot sun in April has caused
A confusion of seasons in our village;
And hiking men are daring an early suntan,
Wearing shorts.

Their knees would like more caution;
Pale and startled beneath new khaki cuffs
They dislike the parade,
Preferring the comfortable, dark cocoons
Of anonymous trousers.

Yet, being the knees of Englishmen
They blush but refuse to bend,
Biding their time; after all, who knows?
Even though Spring has sprung this big surprise
Tomorrow might be Winter.

Why I stopped eating cows

BY PETER MELCHETT

Lord Melchett, politician and Chairman of Wildlife Link, farms in Norfolk.

As a child and teenager I shot birds, watched packs of dogs hunting and killing hares, and killed fish by a variety of unnecessarily cruel means, like a rod and line or speargun. But my attitudes towards animals have changed a great deal in the last 15 years or so.

I hope I enjoyed those pursuits because of the pleasure of being out in the countryside all day, or the excitement of diving underwater, and because of the beauty and variety of the natural world I was in contact with.

Gradually, the killing became more and more incidental, and as soon as I discovered the joys of walking, watching birds and photography, it became unnecessary, and I stopped. I had grown to dislike the inevitable cruelty that blood sports involve, both the trapping, shooting and poisoning of animals that are thought to compete with humans for the pheasants, hares, salmon and so on, and the number of animals wounded, either to be killed later or to die lingering deaths. But I still ate animal flesh, and my dislike of blood sports didn't form part of any coherent view of what rights animals have, or what moral code should govern my relationship with them.

As I became more involved in the politics of conservation and animal welfare, I discovered that many species form strong, lifelong relationships, that some animals may even die of grief if one they are close to is killed. I also learnt that, for many species, being deprived of the opportunity to live in groups, to hunt or forage for food, to mate and give birth, is a living hell. I learnt to see the endless pacing, masturbation and rocking of animals in zoos, not as signs of life, or something to laugh at, but as signs of acute distress.

I stopped eating veal, and felt guilty about the miserable conditions battery hens are kept and die in. As I learnt how the most domesticated pig still wants to live like its ancestors, roaming the forest, rooting, wallowing in mud, and building nests, so I became more and more guilty about the pleasures of bacon, ham and sausages. Intensively farmed pigs and chickens suffer as much or more cruelty than veal calves confined to crates, and usually for longer. I was aware that my views on blood sports, zoos, circuses, veal and eating other animals were becoming more inconsistent year by year....

Then I saw a BBC TV *Horizon* lecture by Professor Peter Singer, an Australian philosopher and the leading exponent of the view that animals have rights. Not identical rights to humans, but rights nevertheless ... I became a vegetarian not because I stopped liking the idea of meat, or the taste, but because I found it immoral. I have no right to do that to animals ...

Wild Life and Tame

LED BY A LAD

It all happened during an extremely cold winter a few years ago. Living where four roads meet, it was unusual for me to see a full-grown swan parading and slipping about right in the middle of the road, which was frozen over like a pond. The commotion caused held-up traffic on all four roads. I placed bread and tasty bits near our gate, hoping the bird would come into the garden; but it resisted all well meant kindness by flapping its huge wings. Motorists were getting fed up; one tried to pass the swan and caught one of its wings. The crowd which had now gathered shouted at him. Someone called the police, which only made matters worse. The swan stayed put, the traffic grew and grew and more people gathered, trying all sorts of means to get it on its way. Then out of the crowd a boy walked right up to the bird. 'Quack, quack, quack,' he said sharply and kept saying it, and to the delight of the crowd the swan followed him. It really was a delightful sight: boy and swan sliding about down the icy lane to open waters nearby. Oh for the wisdom of understanding the mind of a lost swan.   Mrs E Holder, Lancashire

1987

My Friday Farmer

BY ELIZABETH MOORE

The author is a peripatetic farm-secretary, who handles bills, wages, VAT returns, letters, records and accounts for three very different farmers.

Mondays and Thursdays are Farmer White's days. He owns nearly 2,000 acres and grows nothing but corn ... There are no animals on this farm and year after year the yields increase despite neighbouring farmers complaining that the land is being 'corned out'. The fields are almost weedless, the few remaining hedges are properly laid and all the gates hang well.

Nothing ever seems to go wrong on this farm which employs only three men with additional help from contractors with cultivations and harvest. My office is centrally heated, there is an expensive carpet on the floor and I have all the latest office equipment. I seldom see my employer as he sits on many boards and committees and is often away from home ... Whenever I hear the word agribusiness or talk of something being a 'profitable viability', I think of the unsmiling Mr. White with his immensely valuable, joyless acres and

his three dour farm workers.

Wednesday is Farmer Green's day. He owns a 500-acre downland farm of corn, pasture, beef-cattle and sheep. He is in a constant hurry and so is his son who is in partnership with him. Great ruts in the yard and drive are proof of their desperate haste to be gone in their tractors and vans ... Father and son spend much of their time fetching spare parts for their vehicles from the nearby town or driving furiously over the farm looking for each other ... Their stock is moved at high speed too, and I hate to see the tractor roaring behind the wild, frightened beasts ...

I go to Farmer Black on the last Friday in the month and I charge him much less than my other employers. He owns 70 acres of heavy land in the valley and has a small dairy herd. His docile cows are always moved quietly and patiently on foot and Mr. Black milks them single-handed. He always looks tired and despite the tin of

Swarfega on the draining board his hands are stained and rough. My office here is a table in the corner of the large kitchen which always smells of freshly-baked bread. Sometimes it is quite an obstacle course to reach this table, and I pick my way carefully over sleeping kittens, tiny red Wellingtons, a pile of farming magazines and a large basket of clothes waiting to be ironed ... Despite the general untidiness, I am always conscious of an extraordinary air of serenity as I enter the house ...

I was about to go home recently when Mr. Black came in to sign the cheques. As he eyed the bills wearily, he said, 'Sometimes I wonder if it is worth going on.' I am alarmed; he is always tired by tea-time, but I have never seen him depressed before. As if on cue, the rusting Cortina comes slowly into the yard weaving past the dogs and hens ... The little boys tumble out excitedly, followed more slowly by their mother who is carrying two shopping baskets.

I know that they will now all hug Mr. Black unselfconsciously as though they have been away from him for two weeks instead of two hours. In a brief, unguarded moment I see a mixture of pride and love cross his face and I know then that he will always go on. He is far the richest of my employers and the last Friday in the month is my favourite day.

Toll of the Trees

In the small hours of Friday 16 October, the great wind savaged the tall oaks of Guestling Wood, East Sussex, smashing them down on to the sweet chestnut coppice trees beneath. This is a Woodland Trust property where old-style forestry – coppice with standards growing high between them – is practised ...

[Editor's note: Whilst the role of a quarterly is not necessarily to report news, it is surprising that this plea for money from the Woodland Trust is the only reference I could find in The Countryman *to the effects of the Great Storm of 1987. The storm flattened trees across southern England, killed and injured people and animals, severely damaged buildings and left rural areas without power or telephones for days. V.L.P.]*

1988

The train for Arcady

'Scatter,' said Malcolm Moseley to the Rural Life Conference, 'is the essence of rurality. Remove it and you have towns.'

BY HUMPHREY PHELPS

The Hereford, Ross & Gloucester Railway was *our* railway; very few of us who lived within sight or sound of its trains had any doubts on that score. To the regular and the occasional passengers, to those who worked in the fields, that track was part of our world. The little stations were warm centres of rural life: there we met our neighbours, and on the trains those from further afield. When our railway closed almost a quarter of a century ago, a community was dispersed. The camaraderie which the railway had engendered in so many ways was gone; gone like the smoke of its trains which once billowed across our fields. That railway and all its associations were Arcadian …

… By the varying sounds of the trains we forecast the weather; by the sound of the first train of the day we rose from our beds and we returned to them by the sound of the last one. By the trains our days were regulated; by them we knew the times for milking and meals. As the 10.15am came along, the farm-workers had their bait – usually bread and cheese or cold fat bacon. As the 12.40 from Gloucester approached, all along the line field-workers downed tools and donned coats. These were the days when men could be seen working the fields in groups, hoeing or pulling roots, haymaking or harvesting. Working with a rhythm, talking and joking as they worked, made hard work bearable, even enjoyable, just as the sight of the train was enjoyable, too. The end of that style of working and the end of our railway almost coincided – the former so gradually that we hardly noticed it at the time; the latter suddenly.

… It was a steam line to the end. The last passenger train ran on 31 October 1964; a few goods trains used the line for a short time afterwards. Then the track was ripped up with indecent haste – the rails, it was alleged, went to Japan – and the pleasant little stations were obliterated. By and by, most of the ground was sold and the track was no longer even perceptible.

Wild Life and Tame

BADGERED

… My brother, via an aged gamekeeper, suggested we marked our territory the same way as the badgers marked theirs – with urine. Accordingly I patrolled the garden with a plastic bucket, but this operation was only partly successful as late night showers or heavy dew diluted the smell of human urine. On impulse, I decorated the territory markers and all known badger access-points with dollops of half-thawed curry taken from left-overs in the deep-freeze. That evening, about sunset, my husband heard very peculiar noises coming from the spinney bordering a stream below our garden. We have had only one visitation since, from a young male seeking new territory. I doctored his calling card with a pinch of Madras curry powder – and he has dug no more pits in the flower-beds.

Patricia Payne, Old Cleeve, Somerset

DECODING MOLEHILLS

Moles have recently occupied a piece of ground beyond my garden, and I have noticed that the line of mounds that runs for some 50 yards along one side of the field is almost exactly straight. I was reminded of a rainy night in Italy, during the Second World War. My neighbour in the trench was a taciturn, stocky little man who, in civilian life, was employed on a Lancashire estate as a mole-catcher. I clearly remember his assertion that if mole-hills run in a straight line across a field or garden, they have been made by a male mole; if scattered haphazardly over the grass, the female is responsible. Arnold Bosworth, Herne Bay, Kent

In Our Time

I n a break with a long tradition of stability, this period saw several changes
of editor. It seems that the days when the editor of *The Countryman*
remained in his post for at least a decade, if not two, were over. When
Christopher Hall stepped down in 1996, after some 15 years, he was followed
over the next decade by no fewer than four editors: Tom Quinn, David
Wheeler, David Horan and Bill Taylor – five if you include editor in chief,
Terry Fletcher, who kept the seat warm between editors.

Worse, for a while the journal was no longer published 'from the country':
its editorial office was based in London as the twentieth century turned into
the twenty-first. It had been nicely settled in Burford, Oxfordshire, for more
than a half a century, after its first formative 20 years at Idbury Manor down
the road. Fortunately the editorial office was able to move back to Burford
for a year or two, but only as a tenant in Sheep Street, and it moved again
to Broughton Hall, in Yorkshire, and then to Dorset, before finally settling
down at Broughton Hall again. It is perhaps not surprising that editors
succeeded each other in quick succession with all this uncertainty, and the
readers sensed that their old friend was losing its way. There were changes,
too, in the ownership of the journal, and also in its frequency of publication.
From having been a quarterly since its inception, it progressed through
being a bimonthly to a monthly, and also changed from its longstanding and

companionable pocket size to a more modern but unpocketable A5. By 1998 the price per issue was £2.40 – heading towards being 20 times what it had been 70 years earlier, a barometer of how the cost of living had been inflated over the period. By January 2004 the circulation was down to below 26,000.

During this period, new features included 'Corners of Britain', 'Soapbox', 'Tailgate', 'Westminster Book' (by the wickedly perceptive 'Scavenger') and 'The Countryman explores …' series that at one stage became something akin to what might be found in travel guides and tourist brochures, though the aim was to look at different counties – largely from the point of view of the walker – one by one until the entire country was covered. Farmer bashing continued, as farming became more and more remote from the everyday lives of those who read the journal. There was, not surprisingly, much less emphasis on nostalgia and dialect and certainly much less on quirky locals, though the 'Country Characters' series remained loyal to the idea of bringing true countrymen – the 'good old boys' – to life for the overwhelmingly urban readership. There were still some gutsy 'characters' among the regular contributors – men like Robin Page, never afraid to speak his mind on rural matters and with a truly agricultural background, Humphrey Phelps, another with a long and practical experience of farming and the countryside, and Phil Drabble, a true countryman and naturalist. The pseudonymous 'Rusticus' was a light disguise for the rural author of several books in the popular '*Tales of the Old* …' series published by David & Charles in Devon. John Vince continued where his predecessor John Higgs of the Museum of English Rural Life had left off in identifying curious old objects submitted by readers. Peter Marren wrote many a thoughtful article on the environment; Euan Dunn took over as the resident naturalist; and Val Bourne was the gardening expert. Gardening and birdwatching continued to be popular subjects, and came together in 'Gardening for Wildlife'.

A notable change from earlier years, too, was the huge increase in the number of holiday advertisements, which confirmed that, for readers of *The Countryman*, the countryside was more of a playground than a workplace. But there was also a new breed in the villages: urban refugees had discovered that they could indeed work in the countryside, albeit glued to their computer screens and the internet. This new group of incomers was slowly bringing villages to life again: by working from home, they could find the time and desire to be active within their own rural communities. The fields may still have been empty of humans and working horses, replaced by isolated tractor drivers and combines, but the villages were beginning to hum again. On the farms, diversification was the new buzzword, and articles began to appear on unlikely enterprises such as ostrich farming and water buffalo. Passions were stirred when genetically modified crops came on the scene; and they were stirred again at the mention of 'windfarms'.

In the late 1990s there was the first 'Countryside March' in London, and the journal reflected reactions to it by readers and contributors, some of whom felt that the hunting lobby, battling against proposed legislation to ban their sport, had to an extent hijacked the 'countryside' and ignored far more pressing problems that were faced in rural areas: this led to lively debate in the pages of the journal. Old favourites such as antipathy to light pollution, noise pollution, 'new towns', motorways and bypasses continued to be discussed, while a completely new subject for *The Countryman* was the noticeable lack of ethnic minorities living in rural areas.

In 2001, even the most urban readers had the reality of the countryside thrust in their faces by the horrors of the foot-and-mouth disease crisis. The disease had reared its ugly head from time to time throughout the life of *The Countryman* and had always made misery for livestock farmers, but in 2001 television screens and newspapers were relentlessly filled with the sight of huge mountains of burning carcasses and the tearful or stoical faces of those whose animals had been destroyed – often the final nail in the coffin lid on a family farm's hopes for the future. *The Countryma*n reflected the handling of this whole sorry business in articles that were a mixture of despair, anger and sheer incredulity. Depression and suicide rates among farmers rocketed. And for a while, at least, 'farmer bashing' gave way to sympathy. In step with this new rapport, farmers' markets became increasingly popular in towns and cities all over the country.

In September 2007, the year of *The Countryman*'s 80th birthday, its latest editor, Paul Jackson, responded to a readership survey by reintroducing 'perfect' binding and bringing back some of the traditional qualities that had served readers so well in the past, while at the same time reflecting (as the magazine always had) changes in the countryside and in the lifestyles of those who lived in and enjoyed it. Gently *The Countryman* was rediscovering its roots as the 'little green book' that Robertson Scott had conceived in a very different world.

1990

Looking at Nature

by Martin Spray

What colour is green? *When did you last see a coloured face among visitors to your village? As Julian Agyeman, founder of the Black Environmental Network, puts it, we 'lack a black visitor presence in the countryside'. He also points out that of the £20,000,000 or so the Countryside Commission receives in grant, 'virtually nothing is spent to further the interests of about five per cent of taxpayers'. Julian, who is Environmental Education Officer for the London Borough of Lambeth, besides being involved with BEN, is chairman of the Ethnic Minorities Award Scheme for Environmental Projects run by the National Council for Voluntary Organisations. He hopes that separate organisations for coloured people will be temporary, but is clear about the need for a black movement at the moment. He says: 'Globally, environmental problems affect black people disproportionately. In Britain, black people live in some of our worst environmental conditions.' They tend to see rural Britain as 'not for them', and will do so until we show what he calls 'positive images' of people of all colours in the countryside, and don't over-present it as a sort of white, middle-class park.*

No More Eagles

BY CHRIS BRASHER

His name is Pen yr Ole Wen, and my friend Idris Evans, who once kept the village shop in Nant and now ferries the children of the valley to school, knows not what it means except that Pen is the Welsh for Head. He stands at the head of the Nant Ffrancon pass – a massive mountain 3,210 feet high, guarding the route to the coast.

I have been terrified when alone on his flank; I have fished his waters with my brother and caught nothing and that served us right because it was the Sabbath and we were in Welsh-speaking Wales; and I have camped with my two youngest children beside the lake which he embraces between his cliffs.

It was from the coast that I journeyed to him first just after the last war …

Forty-five years later, in January of this year, when the gales had blown themselves out and the sun, climbing into the New Year, gave hope of the spring and of summer warmth, I looked at that steep southern flank of Pen yr Ole Wen … And then I turned east, along the old Roman Road with the ice crunching under my feet, and I thought of this land, the highest land in England and Wales which from time immemorial has been known as Eryri, the abode of the eagles.

Now there are no eagles in Snowdonia. We, supposedly the most intelligent of animals on this planet, have shot them out of the skies. And, in many other ways, we are irreparably damaging their domain.

We want more water to flush down the loo – two gallons per flush. We want more water for the dish-washer and the modern computerised washing-machine. We want more electricity to power these machines. We want wider and straighter roads.

We are like spoilt children whose perpetual cry is 'I want … I want …' If we get what we want now, we may be happy for a moment or two but soon another desire dominates the mind and the cry goes up again: 'I want … I want …'

Somebody has to impose some discipline, somebody has to say a firm 'No'. There is such a person who says

'No' to those who want to defile the wild land of Snowdonia, the land which has refreshed my body and my soul during at least four of the seven ages of man. Her name is Esmé Kirby ... [who] more than 20 years ago ... founded the Snowdonia National Park Society to fight the good fight ...

'The worst defeat was the Cwm Dyli pipeline,' she said. 'The greatest victory is still to come – the A5.'

The pipeline is a hideous wound on the eastern flank of Snowdon ... That mistake must not happen again. We must all join with her in the battle against 'improvements' to the A5 ...

Concerning Conkers

BY JOHN AKEROYD

... Despite the enormous amenity and aesthetic importance of the horse chestnut-tree, the conkers themselves appear to have little economic value. A correspondent in Sussex tells me that he and his wife, tipped off by an old lady from Lancashire, collect conkers each year for their clothes cupboard in order to deter moths. This observation corroborates a recent letter in *The Independent* newspaper noting that people in Russia do the same.

Nevertheless, conkers *have* their uses and they played a curious but significant role in modern history. During World War I, a serious shortage of acetone, a solvent employed in the manufacture of the explosive cordite, caused David Lloyd George, at the time Minister of Munitions, to seek the help of the great Zionist, Chaim Weizmann of Manchester University, who isolated a bacterium that would convert starch to acetone. Forced to abandon maize as a source of starch, due to the reduction in imports caused by German submarines, Weizmann, who was director of Admiralty laboratories, used conkers, apparently very abundant in the autumn of 1917. Collection, mainly by children, was organised nationally (as it was again in World War II), and the acetone shortage was alleviated. Lloyd George in his *War Memories*, noted that this was 'the fount and origin' of the Balfour Declaration, which established in principle a Jewish homeland. Weizmann was to become, in 1948, the first president of the state of Israel.

Personal Call

BY JOHN SHEEHAN

One day in 1948 (or was it '49?) I was on my way to stay with a friend at Brailes in Warwickshire. It was my first visit and I followed his directions closely. When the Stratford Blue bus deposited me in Shipston-on-Stour, I went into the George Hotel as instructed, downed a restorative pint, and went to the telephone which was by a window overlooking the square. The operator at the post office store came on the line after she had finished slicing the bacon or whatever, and the following exchange took place:

Operator: Number, please.

Me: May I have Shipston two-four, please?

Operator: Mister Davis's owt.

Me: Oh.

Operator: Wanna taxi?

Me: Er, yes.

Operator: You'm in the George now, ain' you?

Me: Er, yes.

Operator: Right, lean forward a bit.

Me: Pardon?

Operator: Lean forward – are yer leanin'?

Me: Er, yes.

Operator: Right, now see 'cross the square a lickle notice say Car for 'ire, can't read it where you are but that what it say, tek my word. Put phone on the side an' goo over an' see if 'Arry 'Opkins is there.

I did, but he wasn't. 'Ah,' said the girl, 'fool I am, 'Opkins goo down 'orse sales Fridays, doan 'e?' She then rang Ol' Charlie who was having a row with his wife. Over a fusillade of flying saucepans, he managed to yell 'Not ternight!' and slammed down the phone. 'Oooh, they'm at it agen,' murmured my new confidante, audibly rummaging through her little notebook of hackney carriages *et al*.

She then asked me where I wanted to go. When I told her, she squealed, 'Hey, Ol' Sam goo down Brailes back from the milk run. You'll cop 'im in Banbury Road. You'll 'ave ter run!'

I ran, and I copped him.

PIG-STICKING. At the Bishop Burton College of Agriculture, North Humberside, a Japanese student, Tetsuo Yamashita, is giving pigs the needle. He practises acupuncture on sows to bring them on heat and on boars to improve libido. According to the pig-unit manager (reported in our esteemed contemporary *Pig Farming*), it works.

1992

The old coaching inn in Sheep Street, Burford, that became the editorial home of The Countryman *for half a century.*

Wild Life and Tame

TIGGYWINKLE TIPPLE

One evening a local farmer went to investigate the odd snufflings and squeaks coming from his silage clamp. He couldn't believe his eyes when he discovered a troop of about 20 merry hedgehogs having a party. They'd been lapping the puddles of silage effluent which had gathered on the concrete apron and were in various stages of leglessness, from slightly staggery to flat on their backs, feet waving feebly in the air. They grunted and squeaked as they bumped into each other or the wheels of the tractor. When he went to bring in the cows at 5.30 next morning, not a hedgehog was to be seen, but they were back at their 'local' that night and for several after until the effluent had evaporated.

Helen M. Paterson, Dunblane

1993

Immortality for the Selborne Giant

BY JANE BAKER

I first saw the Great Yew of Selborne in the late summer of 1989 when the generous embrace of its branches brushed the church porch and reached higher than the church tower. A notice declared that its girth was 26ft – an addition of two inches since 1981. The age of yews is notoriously hard to estimate and for this one figures varied from 1,000 to 1,400 years. Whatever the truth, it was still growing.

But on the afternoon of 25 January 1990, gales gusting at 100mph sent the tree crashing across the gravestones. The ancient yew was down.

In the weeks after the fall, students from the arboriculture department of Merrist Wood Agricultural College in Surrey, led by their lecturer John Whitehead, planned to raise the tree and put it back in the ground. The Selborne yew – which Gilbert White mentions in his *Antiquities of Selborne* (1789) – was given a 50–50 chance of survival.

But first a more gruesome task had to be done. The force of the yew's wrenching from the soil had scattered the skeletons of villagers buried around it, leaving bones clutching in its roots like drowning fingers.

… When the excavation was done, the Merrist Wood team supervised the raising of the eight-ton yew which had been dramatically pollarded from 60 ft to a mere 15. … It took a whole day for 11 people, cranes, winches and various other machines to lift and position the yew.

… The next time I visited the Great Yew a few weeks later, its shorn crown and split trunk stood forlornly on a new carpet of turf. Someone had planted primroses around its roots as though the fresh young growth would encourage the yew to survive. All these valiant efforts sadly failed. Last summer, despite meticulous attention from the tree-warden and a watching brief from Merrist Wood, the Great Yew of Selborne was pronounced 'visually dead'.

I went back, reluctantly, early last October. The yew looked at first to be a lifeless hulk with not a sign of green growth. But gradually I began to see it differently.

Here was a magnificent piece of wooden sculpture. The bowl and the whorls and flow of the bark were more beautiful than any work of art. And there was more: within the rotting trunk was a miniature living world of ferns, mosses, bracts, lichen, seedlings and even a sapling. Spiders were spinning webs and small insects scurried about. Around the base, foxglove seedlings were already visible along with a wild honeysuckle that the vicar had been trying to get rid of for years.

The spirit of the Great Yew had changed. Instead of being a symbol of life – a piece of living history – it was now a host to life. Its death was the source of regeneration.

It lives on in other ways too. Carvings are to be made from the largest lopped branches, including a font-cover and a side-altar for the church. Most important a cutting, taken by Merrist Wood during the weeks after the tree was raised, flourished and was planted in the churchyard.

Wild Life and Tame

Hard-backed Houdinis

Anyone who hasn't experienced a close encounter with a tortoise can be forgiven for believing they are slow, unintelligent, cumbersome creatures. However, I challenge anyone to hold this opinion after spending even the shortest of summer breaks looking after our Emma and Horatio. Emma has escaped three times from our garden, which is totally enclosed by a brick wall. A flight of stone steps leads down to a wrought-iron gate which has only three-inch gaps between the vertical bars, four inches narrower than Emma's inflexible shell. We only realised how she did it when we spied her lifting up her short, stumpy legs and whizzing down the steps on her hard, shiny belly like a kid on a tin tray. On reaching the bottom, she neatly turns herself on her side so that she can 'wheel' through the gaps between the bars of the gate. Horatio uses his ingenuity differently. He wedges himself with his back hard against the compost-bin and, with his feet pressed against the wall, successfully 'chimneys' (as rock-climbers say) over the top, usually being lucky enough to land the right way up on a soft flower-bed on the other side. Needless to say, we moved the bin and stretched wire netting across the gate. Since it is only a matter of time before they find some other way of getting out, both tortoises now carry a self-addressed sticky label on their backs. Suzanne Rolfe, Sutton St. Nicholas, Hereford & Worcester

Foxy footwear fetishists ...

I recently made a postal and telephone survey about foxes in Southampton ... Of the 300 or more fox families I discovered in Southampton, some had developed the habit of stealing sandals and training shoes from gardens, sports-grounds, and sometimes from inside houses. At least one was seen coming out of a back door with a sandal in its mouth. Another fox went upstairs and returned with a small child's sandal – the child was asleep on the bed at the time! I found that dens were often lined with sandals, presumably used by the cubs to chew on.
John R. Simms, Shirley, Southampton

1995

One Countryman to Another

An exciting speculation about the cause of that elusive phenomenon – the will o' the wisp – comes to us from Tommy Garnett (a subscriber of very many years in Garden of St Erth, Blackwood, Victoria, Australia).

A FRIEND OF HIS, Fred Silcock, has convinced him that the lights called will o' the wisps come from birds, not from marsh gas. The usual explanation is that marsh gas is ignited so as to appear as a ball of light that hovers or perhaps moves about.

Fred Silcock wrote to local papers all over the Australian continent, enquiring about 'min-min lights', which is what will o' the wisps are called there.

As a result he plotted an enormous number of sightings and advanced the theory that the lights were caused by letter-winged kites. These are mainly white birds and crepuscular in habit. Plagues of rats (*Rattus villosisimus*) in the centre of the continent attract kites; after the plague has died down, the birds disperse widely and Silcock's plots of min-min sightings appear to follow the dispersal paths. But he was unable to find evidence of bioluminescence in the feathers of letter-winged kites.

Tommy Garnett suggested to him that barn-owls might be a source of luminescence; moreover they build up their numbers during plagues of rats and disperse in the same way as kites. Fred was able to find several references in the literature to luminous owls, including this in *The Handbook of British Birds*, edited by H.F. Witherby: 'Rare but well-authenticated instances of Barn-Owls appearing luminous in dark are presumably due to luminous bacteria on feathers, perhaps derived from decayed wood of hollow trees.'

Tommy Garnett also points out that the barn-owl, whose current scientific name is *Tyto alba*, was formerly called *Strix flammea* and the short-eared owl is *Asio flammeus*. *Flammea* and *flammeus* are Latin for fiery or flaming, which seems significant in this context.

He set all this down in a letter to Euan Dunn, our natural-history consultant here and editor of 'Wild Life and Tame', concluding: 'Personally, I am convinced by the evidence that the source of many min-min lights is below the wings of barn-owls (and possibly short-eared owls in Britain and grass owls in Australia).'

[Euan Dunn responds:

... *The Barn Owl* by Mike Read and

Jake Allsop ... gives the background to the most widely accepted explanation that honey fungus, derived from roosting (or perhaps also nesting) in an infected rotten tree, might account for occasional reports of luminous owls (especially the pale undersides of barn-owls). There are several forms of honey fungus and they produce a ghostly greenish luminescence in varying degrees. It is not, however, the fruiting body (toadstool) which glows, but the mycelium which permeates rotten wood. Honey fungus got into many of the timbers used to shore up trenches in the First World War, and soldiers sometimes put splints of glowing wood in their caps so that they could see one another's movements in the dark ...]

Wild Life and Tame

RELIC IN THE SPROUTS

When I lived in St Margarets, near Ware, Hertfordshire, I was digging at the foot of a large patch of Brussels sprouts in late September 1986 when out sprang the most curious insect. It was like a large, fat grasshopper but it had what looked like a little pair of hands at the front of its body. I should have caught it for closer inspection but, instead, I stood spellbound and it scurried away into the sprouts, never to be seen again. When I told my husband, he asked if I had been at the cider.

Betty Robinson, Ormskirk, Lancashire
[A perfect description of the mole-cricket, which is extremely rare in Britain nowadays ... – E.D.]

Farmer's See-Saw

BY JOHN VELTOM

… February brought one of those disasters that must be part of every dairy farmer's nightmare. A gate and safety-chain inadvertently left open to the slurry ramp tempted out an inquisitive troop of cows. The solid pastry-crust surface of the slurry-pit close to the level of the ramp must have looked like a tempting path to freedom. As the cows stepped out they plunged, one by one, into the soft, sloppy morass that is a slurry-pit in late winter. Before the alarm could be raised 11 cows were hopelessly stuck.

My son and I had to act quickly. We rang a plant-hire contractor for a crane and a tracked digger, and we called the fire service animal-rescue section. A full-scale rescue was under way, including coverage by television cameras. We made the regional TV news that evening.

The fire-service men were nothing short of magnificent. They had frogman-type suits which enabled them to immerse themselves in the filth up to the chest. The big hired crane proved to be unmanoeuvrable but one of the fire-service vehicles had a hydraulic lift and sling (normally used for pulling apart crashed cars), with which we were able to raise one cow at a time. With long ropes fixed to two halters, the beasts were then rapidly tractor assisted across to a dirt ramp, hurriedly constructed by the tracked digger, on the other side of the pit. The secret seemed to be to get the cow there before she knew what was happening – and once on a firm footing she was able to walk up to field level. To our amazement, only two or three wanted more than a few moments to recover. They walked nonchalantly back to loose boxes where our vet was waiting to check them over. He advised against hosing them clean, so we rubbed them down with clean straw and some were chewing the cud within half an hour.

MONKISH BUSINESS

SOME YEARS AGO I undertook a land-use survey in the Antrim uplands of Northern Ireland: a wild and beautiful area composed mainly of small, family farms. Looking over a hedge to determine what kind of cattle that farm raised, I encountered the farmer – a small man with a worried look.

'Would you be from the monastery, Sir?' he asked politely.

I don't look particularly holy and I was wearing very un-monkish clothes at the time. I must have looked puzzled by his question, for he went on: 'What I mean is – are you from the Monastery of Agriculture? Have you come specially?'

When I denied any connection with the ministry, his relief was palpable. He immediately invited me to tea with his family. The atmosphere in the house was one of celebration – but, to this day, I have no idea why.

James Voller, Cullompton, Devon

Looking at Nature
BY PETER MARREN

Like, I imagine, many middle-class 'environmentally aware' people in the neighbourhood, one is suffering from a diminished sense of personal worth for not lying down before the chainsaws and bulldozers on the line of the Newbury bypass. But there are so many others who are so much better at this sort of thing, and it seems rather silly to travel by car to a protest about a road. But I did visit one of the protesters' frozen camps after Christmas, and was pleasantly surprised by their welcome, and at their obvious respect for their surroundings. The camps seemed to be separated for dietary reasons. 'We're Ordinary Vegetarians here,' a girl in a magnificent hat told me over a companionable mug of herbal tea. 'Just across the way, where you can hear that coughing, they are the Vegans. And those people over there …', she indicated distant dark hairy figures hunched by the fire, and her voice fell to a hush, '… those people are the Meat-Eaters.'

Whorr, God help the security guards. Some of the tree-dwellers have been there so long that the resident bird-life seems to have accepted them as fellow woodlanders. I have never seen such unconcerned blue tits and nuthatches. They are braver folk than I, Badger, Snowdrop and Dug, up there on the branch, huddled round their stoves as the twenty-first century laps around their tree.

Country Diary

By Humphrey Phelps

The Standard Ferguson, that little grey tractor known affectionately as the 'Fergie' is fifty years old. Fergies soon became a familiar sight on British farms, almost every farmer had one despite the fact that initially they were in short supply. Harry Ferguson, who invented the Fergie, caused a revolution in farming with a system in which implements were an integral part of the tractor.

1996

Small, manoeuvrable and versatile, the Fergie was the product of an inventor of genius, who was also something of an eccentric. Once, while demonstrating one of his early models, Harry Ferguson was disturbed by the noise of the Battle of Britain going on overhead. He objected to the noise they made and telephoned the Air Ministry to re-route them! Later he insisted that all demonstrators of his tractors wear pin-striped suits.

1997

Just Wild About Woodlice

BY ANN TATE

'Woodlouse sauce is equal, if not distinctly superior to shrimp,' wrote the Victorian naturalist, Vincent M. Holt in his book *Why not eat insects?* (1885) ... 'Put into a saucepan a quarter of a pound of fresh butter, a teaspoonful of flour, a small glass of water, a little milk, some pepper and salt. Place it on the stove. Heat and stir. As soon as the sauce is thick, take it off and put in the (boiled) wood-lice. This is an excellent sauce for fish.'

1998

The Magic of Mustelids

BY PHIL DRABBLE

I have been passionately involved with badgers for as long as I can remember and I've done all in my power to shield them from persecution, especially from the obscenity of badger baiting.

When we bought our cottage and 90 acres of adjacent mixed woodland, in 1963, we built an extension to the cottage which we designed as much to be used as a permanent hide, from which we could observe the shy and often endangered wildlife which shared our wood, as for our own personal comfort.

We arrived at the cottage with a sow and boar badger, which I had reared on Lactol puppy food from a bottle since they arrived as naked and blind cubs which had been rescued from badger diggers. I intended to keep them in a secure enclosure, where they would be safe from unwelcome intruders until they were able to adopt our wood as their territory.

The scheme was so successful that our original pair of hand reared cubs grew up to be the focal point of my book *Badgers At My Window* ... The idea also appealed to a BBC producer, for whom I often worked, so he bugged the artificial sett I had constructed using a JCB and a mass of tough roots where intruders could not get at them.

The bugging was sophisticated. A transmitter and microphone were introduced to the sett and wired to a loudspeaker and tape recorder by my study desk. I used to leave the speaker turned on and could tell when both badgers were in the sett from their rhythmic snores. It was a marvellous opportunity to compile an exhaustive glossary of badger noises, and it was wonderful to see the puzzled expression on the faces of fellow naturalists when badger snores or badger conversation interrupted our proceedings.

When our badger returned to his still sleeping mate after a forage in the wood his arrival was greeted by soft whinnies of mutual affection, rather like a stallion's whinny of pleasure. I had no hesitation about identifying the meaning of such greetings because the cubs had so often lavished me with similar gentle welcomes when I had turned up with their bottle to feed them.

I was puzzled for a time because my bugging device also picked up a clicking noise, rather like the noise one would expect when running one's finger down a comb. This noise usually ended with a chattering noise that seemed to indicate annoyance. I realised what this was when Bill Brock, the boar, came in the house and lay on his back to have his tummy rubbed. He would then nibble the hairs along the back of my hand, very gently, as favourite dogs often do. It was this nibbling that caused the clicking I'd heard from the depths of the sett. A number of animals, including cats and horses, groom each other in places they can't reach themselves, and the chitters of annoyance I'd heard were simply the result of the badger being groomed crying out to the badger doing the grooming the badger equivalent of 'Stop. You're pinching me!'

… Stoats and weasels (which

I have also reared) have a lovely, musical crooning affection call, which I also recorded. They are so similar, in looks and habits, that it would not be surprising if their musical affection calls or chitterings of threat and alarm were difficult to tell apart unless the observer knew them well enough personally to put meaning to their language.

… When a friend asked me to play my stoat recordings, I happened to set the tape at half-speed by accident. It shook me to the roots. The reduced speed halved the frequency and lowered the pitch, and it could easily have been mistaken for the affection call of badgers. To confirm my hunch, I played the badger affection call at double speed and, sure enough, we got what the most knowledgeable could have taken as the sonorous 'Come hither' of stoats.

By the purest accident – or carelessness! – I had stumbled on a similarly among *mustelidae* which, so far as I know, had not been recognised previously.

MEAT-EATING MONSTERS

… In America ladybirds are a commercial crop, sold by the bucketful, and raised by ladybird farmers. A one-gallon bucketful contains about 135,000 dormant male and female ladybirds. They are released during spring, just as the blossom opens. They quickly breed and their lizard-like grubs feed on aphids too. The Californian fruit crop was once saved by ladybirds and fruit growers from South Africa, Australia and South America import them from American ladybird farmers …   *Val Bourne*

LETTERS TO  THE EDITOR

Bull riding

Perhaps the young lady who used to ride a bull near Pontefract (High Summer Letters) was probably inspired by similar exploits in the same area by members of the Waterton family. Alice Waterton, whose husband had been killed at the battle of Marston Moor (1644), defended the family home, Walton Hall, against a troop of Roundheads and later harnessed six oxen to the family carriage after Cromwell's men had commandeered her horses. Anne Waterton repeated Alice's trick two hundred years later – with four bullocks – to circumvent the penal laws which forbad Catholics to possess more than two horses. And Anne's son, Charles, when he was still a schoolboy, once rode a cow in the school grounds and later, as an old man, often sat on the flank of his prize bull in Walton Park to feed him with crusts of bread.

Brian Edginton,
West Bromwich

That countryside march

As one who was brought up in a Norfolk village I wish that the Countryside March had concentrated our attention on the real issues. Those who can afford to hunt with hounds and think it right to do so have of course the right to plead their cause as incidentally do those who consider beef on the bone to be an essential part of their diet. But for most country folk the real issues concern the village school, the village shop and post office, the village pub, the village church, the local health centre, the local bus service, prospects for employment; or the lack of such facilities.

Schools, to take one example, depend for their survival and success on the number of children who live in the locality. Children need homes. So the healthy life of the village may well depend on the building of new homes in the area. Most of these should be what is called 'social housing' with the needs of young families particularly in mind. But better off 'incomers' may also play a valuable part in supporting rural causes, not least environmental ones. The countryside's greatest asset is its people.

The Very Rev. A.H. Dammers,
Shirehampton, Bristol

Countryside March

Over the years thousands of small farmers have quit their holdings, small farms have been absorbed into large farms. Farmworkers have lost their jobs. Agri-business in receipt of huge grants and subsidies has denuded rural England. Small trades and rural industries have been forced out of business, country people have no employment and often no house either. Village schools and post offices have closed, in many districts there is no public transport. But all through the long years of Conservative rule there were no marches in London to save the countryside.

Now that hunting is threatened and there is the chance that the public may have the right to free access over mountain, moor and downland, some self-styled champions of the country have sprung into action. The march through London on St David's Day was a great success but I doubt if Lewis Carroll, the late lamented Beachcomber or any satirist could have contrived such a scenario, consisting of absurdities, contradictions and hypocrisy.

There were wealthy landowners, roaming through London determined to prevent the public from roaming across their vast tracts of mostly barren land. By hoodwinking farmers into thinking their farms would be invaded by hordes of marauding townees, they got some farmers to march as well. And with the landowners marched the fox-hunters who want to continue to roam all over the countryside. To add absurdity to contradiction many of the landowners were also fox-hunters and often these are the most vigorous of footpath opponents.

I would have more sympathy with the fox-hunters if only they would be honest enough to say they hunt because they enjoy it, instead of trying to justify hunting by saying it is a tradition (bear-baiting and cock-fighting were also traditions once), or by claiming it provides employment (so does war, drug trafficking or any crime), or that without hunting there would be no foxes or that the country would be over-run by foxes.

I would also have more sympathy with those opposed to hunting if they were as opposed to the larger cruelties inflicted by factory farming methods. It's claimed that 70 per cent of people want hunting banned; if they refused food from factory farms they could soon get these cruelties banned.

They marched, it was claimed, to save the countryside, yet among the number were some who have been steadily destroying the countryside and its wildlife. Agri-business and intensive farming have drenched it with chemical sprays and fertilisers, polluted water courses and the air with stinking slurry, ignored the rules of husbandry and created a landscape without humans. With the aid of massive grants, wetlands, woodlands and hedgerows have been destroyed during the last 40 years; 96,000 miles of hedgerows – enough to go four times around the world – have been lost. As far as I know no-one marched in protest; these latter-day champions of rural Britain certainly did not.

Humphrey Phelps

1999

Skylarks to Australia

by Cyril Bracegirdle

The storm that hit them as they approached the coast of Victoria, Australia, had abated. The wind dropped, clouds rolled away, leaving a sun-warmed canvas of deep blue sea as the *Phillip Van Marnix* eased into its berth at Port Phillip on February 4, 1854.

Robert Morrice, farmer, unloaded his precious cargo of wicker cages which he had nursed throughout the long voyage from England. Seven skylarks remained of the twelve with which he had started.

He rode horseback through Melbourne, the cages strapped to his saddle. Near Geelong, not far from his farm, he stopped and opened the cages. The frail survivors fluttered about for a few minutes, stretching their wings after the long weeks of confinement. Then they rose in formation and flew away into an alien sky.

He watched them go with sadness.

Would he hear their song again? Would they escape the hawks? Would the baking heat of the southern summer be too much for creatures evolved in a milder clime?

… A year passed, then several readers of the *Melbourne Argus* wrote in to say that they believed they had heard a skylark singing. The editor offered 'a one-year subscription to the first reader who can provide authentic evidence on hearing the skylark trilling forth its well known song.'

Within a few weeks a letter came from a gold digger who claimed that he had heard the sweet song of a skylark that reminded him of home in England. The location was about 50 miles from where Morrice had released the birds. Also the digger had not only heard but actually seen one alight.

… The skylark is still heard today in Victoria, Queensland and Tasmania …

LETTERS TO THE EDITOR

Distant noises

In 1787 in Upper Canada, land along the north shore of Lake Ontario was bought from the Ojibwa Indians. The distance along and around the shore – i.e. the amount of land involved – was determined by how far the sound of a gunshot carried from the lake. At that time the distance a man could walk in one day was also use in some treaties.

Douglas Baird,
Ontario, Canada

Kites, screes and free milk

I refer to a letter from Graham Tavistock – 'Bring back school milk' [which] mentioned the waxed cardboard bottle-tops and the use to which the girls put them [for making woollen bobbles]. He failed to mention the use boys made of them. If they were threaded onto a kite string they would start to vibrate, with the thrumming of the string, and gradually work their way up the string to the kite. I have no idea of the physics behind this phenomenon. We would compete to see who could get the most bottle-tops up to the kite.

Charlie Ablethorpe,
Leigh-on-Sea, Essex

TENORS IN DECLINE

The decline of rural communities has some curious consequences and not just in Britain. In Italy there is a worrying shortage of young tenors – the opera houses cannot it seems recruit anywhere near the numbers they need. The reason? Most seem to agree that as agriculture in Italy has declined and fewer young men work on the land, so there is less singing. 'Rural solitude inspired people to sing,' says one historian of music, 'but today they work in offices and listen to music on tapes and CDs.'

Tom Quinn

Tin Tabernacles

by Laurence Dopson

For 92 years people worshipped in the iron mission church of Holy Trinity, Street, Somerset. But then it began to sink. That is the trouble with 'tin tabernacles'. Intended as temporary buildings they are, by their nature, a dying breed. There are, however, survivals yet, just as at Greensted, Essex, there is a wooden church which has survived from Saxon times. On the royal estate in Norfolk there is even a thatched tin tabernacle at Babingley.

The squire, George Wickstead of Shakenhurst, gave £10 in 1895 to start the subscription list for the iron church which still provides the inhabitants of the hamlet of Clows Top with 'nearer access for Divine Worship than either of the parish churches' in this neck of Shropshire, as the Archdeacon of Ludlow remarked at its dedication a century ago. The MP, father of Prime Minister Stanley Baldwin, contributed, so did 147 people altogether, 34 donors gave 6d and four 3d each. The total cost was £70 18s. The Bishop's licence stipulated that the altar should be curtained off when the building was used for village tea parties. The fact that it was a tin tabernacle on a hill proved an unexpected advantage. Parishioners were able to start the Revd. W. Winnington-Thomas's Austin 7 for him in the '50s by pushing it down the slope.

Tin tabernacles are an important if brief and overlooked episode in the history of church architecture.

Iron church advertised for £340 in Boulton & Paul's 1900 catalogue.

'The first was built in London in 1855 and their period is the end of the 19th century up to the Great War,' says John Bracey, who has made a study of them. 'I believe that tin tabernacles should be recognized as listed buildings, particularly as examples of prefabrication.'

Many of the tabernacles in the east of England, particularly in Norfolk, were supplied and constructed by the internationally known and well established Norwich engineering firm of Boulton and Paul. 'Although not so artistic or good looking as wood, iron churches are at the same time quite as serviceable, while the cost is less,' they stated frankly in their 1902 catalogue. 'With an interior lining of felt and match-boarding they are absolutely free from damp, and are warm in winter and cool in summer.' …

Country Diary

By Humphrey Phelps

1999

A man whose word I trust told me that he was present on a dairy farm at milking time when a man from Tesco arrived. Wearing a white hat, white coat and white gumboots he'd come to inspect the milking. It wasn't long before some cows, as cows will, especially when a stranger appears, lifted their tails and dunged. And while out on grass, cows, as we say, can be very 'loose'. The inspector was horrified, he protested loudly, thus causing more cows to lift their tails and perform. 'This is dreadful,' he said, 'we can't allow this to happen where food is being produced.' 'Well,' said the cowman, 'it's something that happens on every dairy farm every day and I don't know what you or I or anyone else can do about it.'

2000s

THE NEW MILLENNIUM

Nearing 90

BY PHIL DRABBLE

My wife Jess and I are both nearer 90 than 80. We celebrated our diamond wedding anniversary, that's 60 years in case you didn't know, last September and like you we have reached the third millennium. In our case, of course, it might be said – given our ages – that we have done it by the skin of our teeth.

Of course these days to be old is to be part of a huge and increasingly powerful section of the community. The grey market, they tell us (by 'they' I mean the marketing whiz kids), gets bigger every year. And if we are to judge by those currently mapping out the whole pattern of human genes (the human genome project) anyone reaching the age of 90 at the end of the next millennium will probably be considered a mere youngster.

But for now, chaps like me are obviously approaching the time when we will tumble off our perches. Despite this unavoidable fact I don't really think I would choose to be a youngster rather than an Oldie. I should not like to think of beginning life again now when the world faces such an uncertain future. I can look at the problem dispassionately because it so happens that in our long and happy life together Jess and I had no children of our own.

The biggest change in attitudes over my long life has been a move from general deference for certain individuals and institutions to a cynical questioning of almost everyone and everything in authority. We may have over-done the forelock tugging in the past but these days we seem to have gone to the other extreme and we blackguard everything – including, I am sad to say, the Royal Family. It is probably unfashionable in some quarters to be an ardent royalist as I am, but I can't help thinking that without the Royal Family life would be that bit less interesting. They contribute to the gaiety (difficult word to use these days) of the nation.

But away from all the political

arguments and rows about how the country should be run there have always been for me pleasures that provide the perfect antidote to a stressful life. Take the birds that come to feed by the windows of our house. What greater pleasure than to watch them from the window as they hover and twist, dart and dive. All day they come – tits and collared doves, wagtails and woodpigeons. I am as close to them as I would be in a zoo yet they are free. *[Editor's note: Phil Drabble died in 2007, aged 93. V.L.P.]*

Comment

IN THE DEPTH of the foot and mouth crisis it is difficult to look beyond the next news bulletin or the next statistical milestone. As I write this column the number of confirmed cases has just passed the 1,000 mark. The only certainty is that by the time you read it that figure will be worse. The great unanswered question is just how much worse? Behind each statistic is a story of flocks and herds killed, lives and livelihoods shattered. Yet even that does not convey the complete picture. Like an iceberg, the visible part represents only a fraction of the whole. Around those confirmed cases are thousands of other farms where stock has been slaughtered as part of the precautionary 'firebreaks' and beyond them is another ring of families desperately hoping that the virus will not come nearer and that their animals will be spared.

Yet even that does not tell the whole story. As the crisis deepened and the ripples spread, more and more people have been hit. Tourism, nowadays a staple of the rural economy, was quick to feel the effects in the shape of cancelled bookings in hotels and B&Bs. Behind them came the other attractions and the shops which depend on free-spending visitors to keep going. Next came the support services, some of which may not have even realised that they were part of a tourism economy nor how interdependent agriculture and tourism had become.

There have been a handful of largely isolated, strident voices in both groups. On one side we have heard from farmers who have demanded that the countryside should be completely quarantined and visitors turned away no matter what cost to tourism, while on the other the occasional hotelier has urged a complete opening up of the countryside with the disease allowed to run its course. Thankfully the majority have supported a more pragmatic line which will allow both sectors to be protected while causing the minimum of damage to the other. *Terry Fletcher, editor in chief*

The Tragedy Could Have Been Avoided

by Robin Page

It is difficult to write about a tragedy, but in the circumstances I have no option ... During the course of the current epidemic I have had farming friends almost completely surrounded by the disease; life for them has become a time of tension and torment. I have had telephone calls too from complete strangers, they have had the disease and their voices have been full of despair, disbelief and anger. For them the summer fields are empty; there are no lambs, no calves and for some there seems to be no future and no hope. The year 2001 will linger in the language of farming folklore; that is if there are any farmers left in 30 years time to remember and talk about times past.

To me the scenes we have witnessed over recent weeks and months are unforgettable and unforgivable; a controllable disease with little lasting impact on the animal it affects, in a modern, First World country, has been regarded as a cruel scourge and treated in a way that can only be described as medieval. Thousands upon thousands of good, healthy animals have been massacred and burnt as if part of some primitive Satanic ritual. Funeral pyres have been seen smouldering for days; piles of uncovered bodies have been left at roadsides and human feelings have been totally disregarded as the politicians have recited their favourite, empty and meaningless mantras, 'the slaughter policy must continue' and 'we have the outbreak under control'.

In the middle of all the mindless Ministry-induced claptrap and mayhem I received a telephone call from a friend who lives in Kenya. 'What is going on in England, Robin?' he asked. 'Have the politicians lost the plot? I worked on a farm in Kenya in the 1950s which developed foot and mouth. The old Colonial Service vets came out and said "Leave it and it will quickly be over." Within a month it had swept through the entire herd and we only lost two animals. Most just suffered minor discomfort and the biggest problem was when a cow with a calf went dry and had no milk. Foot and mouth may be a highly contagious disease, but it is not a serious problem.'

... Despite the self-congratulation of some politicians and officials, the way in which this foot and mouth outbreak has been handled has been nothing short of scandalous ...

LETTERS TO THE EDITOR

Flexible farming

A dear friend from Dorset has sent *The Countryman* to us for many years. As farmers and lovers of our New Zealand fauna and flora, we are always intrigued at the lessons we can learn from your experiences, both happy and unfortunate, and how they can relate to our endeavours. Lessons like these travel both ways.

Thus, I've been fascinated with the debate in the UK about possible removal of farm subsidies. Ours ended totally and abruptly, without warning, in 1984. There was doom and gloom, with forecasts of thousands of bankruptcies. As it turned out, only a few hundred succumbed, most of whom were probably already on the slippery slope. The reaction was to farm strictly to the demands of the market, rather than to the demands of the political masters. Everyone adjusted, in the flexible way most farmers can, and now you would be extremely hard put to find anyone advocating any subsidies.

One of the unexpected side results was the impact on conservation and care of the land. No longer were farmers exhorted by price signals to farm every last acre, even if it was marginal economically. 'Bush' (tall forest to you!) was left unfilled, steeper slopes no longer forced into grazing where it was better in trees.

It is inspiring to find, for example, farmers planting areas in native trees with no commercial value, just to encourage the presence of indigenous birds like the tui, bellbird, or kereru.

Perhaps the deepest change, often not recognised, has been the realisation that 'there is no more land', so what we have had better be managed sustainably if a living is to be had. Over the last ten years in particular, there has been a remarkable change in attitude to the importance of such esoteric issues as biodiversity, and its role in good land management.

So the message I would have for fellow farmers in the UK is to accept the rather frightening prospect of life without subsidies, to meet the challenge, and you will thrive on it after the traumatic first few years. I sincerely wish you well.

Gordon Stephenson,
Putaruru, New Zealand

Curiouser and Curiouser

by John Vince

Splarging Explained

In October, we asked if anyone knew how to splarge a well. Derek Holmes, a retired surveyor of Leeds, has told us that splarging is a term derived from pargetting and plastering. There seems to be a suggestion that splashing about, with plaster, also helped in the formation of this unusual word.

When the wall of a well needed attention it had to be carefully inspected by a builder who, armed with a miner's helmet and lamp, climbed down a secured ladder to examine the condition of the steening (the wall). If this needed repair, the joints in the masonry were raked out and a layer of lime mortar, about an inch thick, was applied.

In Scotland the word splarging is still in use and it has, so Bob Smith of Linlithgow says, four different meanings.

> " *'I feel very proud of my ancestor,' said one man to another. 'Probably,' came the reply, 'but how would your ancestors feel about you?'* "

Enough to Make Grown Men Cry

BY JO COLLINGBORN

Recently, a farmer friend of mine made a startling revelation, as we sat at the kitchen table. He told me that on a routine visit to the doctor he had suddenly broken down and sobbed his heart out. I was absolutely amazed, not only that it happened but also that he had told me. I have known him all my life; he is a strong, silent, successful farmer whom I imagined would cope with anything that life threw at him.

As we sat and analysed the situation, we decided that a farmer today is like the captain of a ship in a continuing storm, who must not show any signs of weakness or doubt in his ability to cope, for fear of spreading panic among the crew, i.e. his family and staff.

Running a family farm today is like trying to steer a runaway car with no brakes down a steep, bendy hill. You are just about coping but don't know where it will end and suspect the next raft of legislation and bureaucracy that is about to come around the next corner may be something that you are unable to negotiate.

This farmer had subconsciously acknowledged within the privacy and professionalism of the doctor's surgery he could give release to feelings that even he himself did not know existed. Farmers have seen themselves slowly dribbled into a situation not of their own making. Always in the past, if you hit a bad year due to weather or low prices, you would farm through it waiting for better times.

The past five years have been a continual downward spiral, with the latest insult being the supermarkets raising the price of milk by 2 pence a litre and stating that this rise must go back to the farmer. This is purely window dressing by the supermarkets, as we have been informed that when we receive this it will only be 0.77 pence per litre.

When in the history of commerce has a supermarket buyer voluntarily increased his purchase price? They appear to be acknowledging that the sheer abuse of their buying power has put farmers in a situation where they can no longer cope financially or emotionally.

A friend working in the counselling service recently commented that foot and mouth came along just in time because it enabled farmers to admit they needed help. Today the foot and mouth has gone away but the farmers' problems haven't.

LETTERS TO THE EDITOR

Wind industry

As a long-time reader (some time pre-war) I have been most interested in the correspondence on windfarms. It is quite wrong to call them 'farms'. They are industrial units placed in rural settings and unfortunately in some of the most beautiful places.

As some of your correspondents say, they are not efficient and they certainly do not beautify their setting. They are a political attempt by the Government to show the urban population that they are doing their bit to save the planet, but not caring that they are damaging the best of the countryside.

The principle of clean power is good, but windfarms have to be where the wind is, and that nearly always is in the most beautiful and isolated places which are rapidly being eroded.

As a small landowner in a beautiful part of North Wales, the Ceiriog valley, we were informed of a proposal to erect three 300ft wind turbines less than a mile away on the top of the hill making them visible for miles around. The valley residents erupted and, despite a sparse population, arranged a protest meeting at which 500 people filled the hall. Many signatures were collected, and later a committee produced reasoned local arguments against the proposal which was eventually rejected by both the planning authority and the Wrexham Borough Council. Unfortunately it is possible that it will rear its ugly head again in a different form.

David Pick,
Llwynmawr, nr Llangollen,
Wrexham

Ban Farming ... I Want to Live a Little Longer

by Robin Page

Ban farming; yes I know some readers will be shocked, but at last I agree with the Government; farming should be banned. Although I agree with the sentiments of our lovable urban politicians, my reasons for wanting the ban are very different. Our politicians, it seems to me, want to turn the countryside into theme parks, where the few rustics left can get jobs washing up in quaint country pubs or they can pick up litter around 'picnic area' car parks. Some will be required to sit on walls wearing smocks and chewing straw, to add an air of authenticity to the holiday home residents, the second homers and, in the case of MPs, the third and fourth homers.

Farming in such a theme park holiday haven could be noisy, dirty and a health hazard, so if farming was banned the field could be mowed instead of grazed; Tibetan chimes in the trees or suspended by the patio would be a much better sound than the barking of sheep dogs or the mooing of cows and without combine harvesters and balers the countryside would be much quieter and cleaner.

Sooner or later there is almost bound to be a European directive ordering all fields and footpaths to be hoovered twice a week, to remove all obnoxious droppings from the countryside – from cow pats to otter spraints – and so the fewer animals in the countryside, wild and tame, the better.

My reasons for banning farming are completely different; but the overall effect would be the same all the farms in Britain would be closed down. The truth is that farming is much too dangerous, and so for health and safety reasons farms should be shut. The alternative would be for a health and safety officer, a hygienist, a physiotherapist, a paramedic and a personal trainer to be assigned to every person working on the land.

Their task would be to identify every hazard and advise how to overcome them. They would give out plastic gloves or medicated wipes every time an animal was touched. They would recognise hazards, such as conkers on the ground, rabbit holes, and fallen leaves on the path. If fallen leaves can disrupt the whole railway system think about the many autumn dangers on the farm.

My sudden change of tack follows a sudden change of direction.

One second I was climbing up a ladder to get some hay and straw for the cows; the next minute I was hurtling downwards, head-first, towards the concrete floor of the Dutch barn. I am happy to report that I did absolutely no damage to the concrete floor but in breaking my fall with my right arm I very nearly broke my arm and, as I type, it is still very painful.

In addition I managed to crack my head. If I had been a spring board diver I think I would have received 9.5 marks out of 10 for content and 1.2 for presentation.

… The whole incident made me think of all the near misses I have had on the farm – and there have been many. The worst was falling out of a willow tree with the chainsaw locked on full throttle … Then there was the stroppy cow with the calf. One minute I was bending over the calf putting in an ear tag, the next minute I was flying through the air as the mother hit me at speed from behind … Machinery! Oh where do I start? … And these are only a sample of my farming horror stories; so yes, ban farming. I want to live a little bit longer please.

Dotcom Farmers Do it Differently

BY JO COLLINGBORN

Although we live 15 miles away from Swindon, which was the fastest growing town in Europe, not in population figures I might add, but in sheer area, we are still not far enough away to avoid the appearance of a plethora of 'pony paddocks'. These are small parcels of land sold off by individual farmers to raise some much needed cash, to subsidise the continuation of the main farming business. This modern phenomenon is to satisfy the need of the individual to own a piece of land to put his hand on, and also to indulge his daughter's

" THE SIGN IS UTTER NONSENSE, SIR –
THEY STOPPED LAYING A WEEK AGO"

whim for a pony. We are also seeing an influx of dotcom people, who buy a whole farm for the sake of the farmhouse and then wonder what to do with the land. These arrivals are causing a great change to the local landscape.

It's interesting to observe these newcomers' attitude to the land they acquire. First, on goes the padlock, next, the sign 'Private Property Keep Out'. This, we farmers find infuriating. We know the fields we own, we know the fields they own and we wouldn't dream of going on their property without their permission, or conversely, are they suggesting that theirs is the only private property in the area and that ours is therefore open to the public? Whenever I get the chance, I teasingly remark with all this security, are they afraid we're going to sneak in at night and roll the field up and take it away?

Much of the sale of these small parcels of land for pony paddocks is a welcome opportunity to improve the cash flow of the struggling family farms around here, the majority of new owners seem to lose interest after three years and the land goes back on the market to be acquired by another aspiring pony paddock purchaser, so therefore, it will never go back

into agricultural production. I am undecided as to the merits of these particular operations but I sometimes despair of the whole countryside disappearing under pony paddocks.

The dotcom farmers are different. As long as they arrive in a Rolls Royce and leave in a wheelbarrow at regular intervals, we are quite happy. They spend about two years piling money in to improve their farms, and show us how it should be done, followed by a year of quiet reflection when most accept that you can't beat nature, you have to farm with the weather. It doesn't matter if a tractor's got four-wheel drive, or eight-wheel drive, you can't beat wet clay. Most often they then let their land out for their neighbours to farm.

The clever dotcoms do the reverse. When they arrive, they let their land out for three years to their neighbours, watch how it's done and then quietly take the land back in hand and become reasonable farmers. It's interesting that in general the successful newcomers or 'new landers' are happy to seek advice, which is happily and freely given. Generally those who fail come in with grandiose ideas that they are going to knock farming into the 22nd century. Nearly always, the farm wins.

Days Numbered for the Grid Relics of the Past?

BY ROGER FREE

Earlier this year, as I was walking the Dorset lanes from Corfe Castle towards the coast at Kimmeridge, my travelling companion was enthusiastically reporting the information relayed to him by satellite on his Global Positioning System device. Here we were, now, he would tell me, at grid reference so-and-so; half a mile on, and we were now at so-and-so reference. As we approached the next turning, and having made it clear I was not looking over his shoulder at his GPS, I mentioned casually that we were now at grid reference 916811.

My companion checked his screen. Yes, he agreed, with a mixture of surprise and slight irritation (he loves such gadgets) – but how, he demanded, could I have known. The answer, there and at many a rural junction in Dorset, is that the traveller simply glances at the finger-post. Above the arms indicating distances and destinations will be seen a hollow ring, properly referred to as an annulus, bearing the name of the junction, and also its six-figure grid reference.

Having moved to Dorset fairly recently, and keen to learn more about this useful provision, my first source of information was Mike Browne, not long retired from the Highways Department. He spoke with pride of the way in which the County Council had sought to perpetuate these unusual map reference signs, though unfortunately some had been lost during the war, when they were removed to confuse any invader.

… Among Dorset's black and white grid-referenced finger-posts there can be found some painted bright red. They carry the same information, and the reason for the colour is much debated. One theory is that these posts served as markers for men on the march, indicating where food and overnight accommodation might be found. Such travellers might have included prisoners who, with their guards, were on their way to the docks, under sentence of transportation … In other counties, such as Devon and Somerset, similar posts are known as red posts but are not so coloured …

R.I.P.: Only a Rabbit

BY GLYN FREWER

Why am I writing this down? I'm not Saint Francis, yet the poignancy of the event sits on me like a judgement. Yet what else could be done? It started on a glorious spring morning, and the rabbit was grazing at the end of the lawn. I looked half an hour later and he bounded leisurely to the flower bed. I decided I had provided him with enough hospitality and it was time to shoo him away. I expected him to run, white scut bobbing, but he ignored me. He was blind, his eyes bulbous protruberances, closed and disfigured by mxyomatosis. How I hate this disease; its slow disfiguring, disabling grip on the animal's sight and brain and nervous system appals me. And there's no cure. So I walked away, telling myself that Nature knew best and would take its course. I thought of killing it myself, for he was surely doomed, but he was nibbling cow-parsley and sunning himself and I couldn't do it.

I saw him next, crouching in the orchard, only his heaving flanks giving signs of life. He looked a poor wretched creature and I wondered how I would kill him. Hit him on the head with a rock? Put a sack over him and hit him hard without looking and hurry away? Again I decided, seeing him look so sick, to let Nature do it for me, but I felt cowardly, for this animal had no quality of life left and the sooner it was over, the better.

That evening, when I had drawn the curtain across the glass French doors, I heard a thud into the glass door. In the past, a blackbird, chaffinch and blue tit had done it, falling stunned to the gravel, reviving in a few seconds and flying off apparently none the worse. I drew the curtain but there was no bird. It was the rabbit. I had last seen him 100 yards away. His blind course had led him to knock on the door four feet from where I was sitting. If ever I had come across a providential cry for help, this was it.

Now I had to do something. I donned gardening gloves, picked him up and decided to take him to thick undergrowth surrounding a fallen willow in an adjacent field. There he could die in peace, in shade, screened from predators. I realised this was not answering a cry for help at all. This rabbit wanted his life to end because it had become unbearable. He had knocked on my door and here I was doing something that would prolong it. I still couldn't bring myself to kill him but I knew now what I had to do. I put him in a cardboard carton. He made no effort to wriggle and no sound. He knew as well as I did. I drove to the vet and handed over the carton, mumbling that she must think me very weak-minded and squeamish. She assured me I was not so, but I was unconvinced.

I went home wondering and probably always will wonder. What led that blind dying creature a hundred yards in my direction and having found me, do the only thing possible to gain my attention, knock on my door? How could he have possibly done that on purpose? Fanciful? Of course it is. But isn't it nice to have such fancies?

Westminster Notebook

by Scavenger

Unwelcome face of rural 'apartheid'

Are country folk racist? Trevor Phillips claims they are. He says black and Asian families are forced to live in big cities because when they stray into rural parts they are subjected by locals to 'a passive form of apartheid'.

Mr. Phillips, a black broadcaster turned chair of the Commission for Racial Equality, speaks from personal experience. He says that on his own countryside forays, 'You go into the shop and people look at you as if to say – "Where have you come from, Planet Zarg?"'

He raises an important issue. There are reports of ethnic minority ramblers and sightseers receiving a less-than-warm welcome, while the far-right BNP has even picked up votes in idyllic village wards.

Mr. Phillips points out that many black and Asian immigrants come from rural backgrounds. He has some useful ideas for bonding, such as promoting a shared love of cricket – played in the West Indies and on English village greens alike.

Index

Aaron's Wish 81
acupuncture 188
acrodrome footpaths 43
aeroplanes 16–17
  see also Country House
  aeroplane
agribusiness 168
agriculture 10, 34, 69, 165
Agyeman, Julian 185
Akeroyd, John 187
Alderney 72–3
Aleppo 15
ancestors 210
angling 19–20
Ansford, Isabel 113
Answers to Correspondents 71
Anti-Litter League 39
apartheid, rural 218
Arcady, train for 180
Archers, the 90
army land 120

artificial insemination 104, 156
As a Farmer Sees It 118–9, 126–7, 139, 156
As It Seems To Some Of Us 10, 14, 58, 6, 73, 77, 89, 120
As One Countryman To Another 10, 16, 82, 123
ATS girls 63
Attlee, Clement 49
Autogiro 21

badgers 181, 198
Bailey, Hon. Lady 18
Baker, Jane 190
Baldwin, Earl 75
Baldwin, Stanley 8, 12
Balfour, Lord 14
barns 78
barrage balloons 58
barter 74

Barwick's follies 107
Bates, HE 35
Beeching, Dr 100, 145
Bennett, Jeremy 154
Beresford, Tristram 101, 118–9, 126–7, 139
billhooks 167
bird-scarers 90
birds 33, 121, 140–1, 193
  as food 58, 63
  as lighthouse casualties 40–1
  hypnotised 106
blackcurrants, planting 149
bluebells 124
Blumenfeld, RD 48
bombs/bombers 51, 170
Bourne, Val 183, 199
Bracegirdle, Cyril 202
Brasher, Chris 186–7
breast-feeding 58
breeds, cattle 156

Broughton Hall 182
Brown, AH 28
bulls 51, 75, 80, 157, 200
Burford 68, 182, 189
Burra, JAN 92
Bush, Raymond 9, 51, 54, 58, 60, 63, 65, 74, 76, 79, 87, 89, 91
bypass protesters 196

Cadburys 36, 64
calving 83, 175
Campbell, Bruce 69, 116, 128
camping 116
camps, ex-wartime 82
cancer cure 97
car numbers 46, 100
Carson, Rachel 101, 114
caterpillars 74
cats 108, 115
caviar 91
Cerne Giant 22
Chamberlain, Neville 33
chemurgy 52–3
chestnuts, horse 187
chicken tenderizer 71
Christian, Garth 80
clocks 87, 112
Cochrane of Cults, Lord 48
cock's stride, daylight and 84
Cole, Dora A 133
Collingborn, Jo 211, 214–5
Common Market 100
computers 183
conservation 161
Cooper, Barry 157
Coren, Alan 162–3
Cornish, vernacular 93
Cornwallis, RK 114
coronation 69, 87
Council for Preservation of

Rural England 44
Country Diary 197, 201, 205
Country House Aeroplane 9, 18, 21
Countryman, The
    advertisements in 36, 183
    anniversaries of 75
    cover of 101, 125, 151
    editors of 6–7, 68, 125, 151, 182
    offices of 182
    see also Burford; Idbury
    price of 10, 68, 101, 125, 151, 183
    sales/circulation figures for 10, 36, 183
    size of 10, 36, 183
Countryman Club 9, 29, 62, 71, 76, 78, 84, 88, 97, 106, 108, 119, 128, 129, 149
Countryside March 184, 200, 201
cows 63, 64, 95, 133, 146–7, 195, 214
crabs, poaching with 83–4
Creech Hill 166
Creswell-Evans, Jane 140
cricket 144–5
Cripps, John 68, 101, 125
Cripps, Sir Stafford 49, 68, 75
Cruel Sports, Society for Prevention of 17
cycling 63
cystus gum 32

Davies, DJ 146
DDT 63
deaf aid, dog and 87
decimalisation 125
deer 173
Denham, Dr HJ 27

dentists 32
deprivation, rural 160–1
Devon, vernacular in 105
distilling, illicit 74
diversification 184
Dopson, Laurence 204
doctors, rural 67
dogs 87, 106, 169
donkeys 110, 157
Down on the Farm 168
Downing Street garden 33
Drabble, Phil 183, 198–9, 206–7
drivers, courtesy 130
dung, as post plaster 108
Dunn, Euan 183, 193–4
Dunsterville, Maj. Gen. LC 48–9
Dutch elm disease 149

Eaden, Ruth 96
eagles 186
EEC 125
eel blobbing 94–5
eggs 41, 47, 214
    brooding 74, 78
electrocution 47
electric fencing 63
electricity 71
elephants 67
Elizabeth, Princess 73
    see also coronation
Ellis, HF 130–1, 135, 174
energy, renewable 52–3
Englishmen's knees 175
Enklefield, legend of 170–1
environment 123, 125, 135
Epistles from an Old Homestead 30, 43, 46, 50
Ervine, St John 24
ethnic minorities 184, 185,

218

evacuees 50, 51
Evans, Simon 43
ewe, cow-herding 95
exploitation, animal 126–7
eyes, reflections from 20

faith healing 149
false tongue 57
farm secretaries 178–9
farmers 53, 211
  dotcom 214 5
  see also As a Farmer Sees It
Farmer's Ruminations 70,
  90, 104
farming 211
  factory 139, 201
  future of 26–8
  German 65
  hazards in 213–4
  in New Zealand 209
  subsidies and 209
  see also agriculture
Ferguson, Harry 97, 197
Festival of Britain 69
fingertip, chopped-off 88
fforde, P 83–4
fish manure 32
Fletcher, Terry 182, 207
fog horns 111
follies 107
foot-and-mouth disease 60,
  184, 207, 208
Forman, Joan 94
fox-hunting 16–17, 69, 201
foxes 61, 86, 169, 192
Free, Roger 216
French words 62
Frewer, Glyn 217–8
frogs, screaming 109
From Day to Day 38

fruit, storage of 41
Fruit Grower's Diary 9, 32, 39,
  41, 47, 51, 54, 58, 63, 74, 79,
  87, 89, 91
fuel crisis 143

garden, cook's dream 150
gardeners 15
Garrett, Armorel 95
geese 90
Gibbs 55
Gill, Crispin 125, 140, 143,
  151
glow-worms 89
Green Belt 117
Grenville, RH 115
grid references 216
Grigson, Jane 150
guinea-pigs 128
  rats and 80, 92 3
gunshot, as measure of
  distance 203
gypsy ear-rings 94

Hall, Christopher 145, 151,
  182
Hall, Sir Daniel 27, 35
Hargreaves, Harry 166
harnts 79
Hart, Edward 142
hay-fever 129
haystacks, Indian 102
hawkers 110
Heath, Edward 136
heating, underfloor 119
hedgehogs 189
Helgoland 30–1
helicopters 70
hens 65, 113
Higgler 14
Higgs, Clyde 70, 90, 101, 104

Higgs, John 183
Highlands 44–5
Hillaby, John 172
hills, dangerous 113
hives, transporting 62
hobby, chaffinch and 85–6
Home Acre 35, 42, 62
Homer Hawkins, AJ 29
honesty 86
honey fungus 134, 194
Horan, David 182
horse-riding 162
horses, working 22
horseshoes 122
hullaballoo 120
Hume, Major CW 77
Hunkin, Gladys 93

Idbury 8, 68, 101, 182
In the Country and Out of It
  10, 65, 97
Introducing Britain 59
Island, In Search of an 37,
  40–1

Jackson, Paul 184
Jamaica 79
Japanese bath 12
Jeff, R 92–3
Jennings, Jack 155, 159
Jerred, Richard 170–1
jizz 128
John, Humphrey 30, 43, 46, 50

Keeble, Frederick 25
Kennington, Eric 48
kites
  children's 203
  letter-winged 193

ladybirds 199

lambs 15, 148
land girls 56
land workers, percentage
of 38
leg pains 75
Letters to the Editor 200, 203,
209, 212
lighthouses 40–1
Lillie, Dr Harry R 77
lily cure 106
Lindsay, HA 103
Lloyd George 12, 14
Lockley, RM 30–1, 37, 40–1,
72–3
Long, Dr Alan 167
Lynmouth disaster 91
Lyth, Phyllis 108

MacDonald, Ramsay 12, 13,
14, 15, 38, 75
maggot breeding 54, 166
Marren, Peter 183, 196
McDiarmid, Norman I 83
McNeillie, John 46
meat-eating 176–7
Meek, Victor 110
Melchett, Lord (Peter) 176–7
mergansers 155
MERL 183
Merrist Wood Agricultural
College 190
mice 112
milk bottle tops 203
milk sterilization 25
milking 58, 81, 158, 205
Milligan, Spike 164–5
min-min lights 193
mole-crickets 194
mole gun 174
molehills 181
Monastery of Agriculture 196

Moore, Elizabeth 178–9
Morrice, Robert 202
motorbikes 166
Motoring Tales, Readers' 10,
20, 64, 119, 121
Mountbatten, Philip 73
mouse, frozen 74
mouse traps 55
mule racing 99
Murrain 60
mustelids 198–9
myxomatosis 32, 69, 89, 217–8

Nairn, Ian 137
National Park 44–5
New Forest 47, 162
new towns 117
New Zealand 209
night 20, 142
nightjars 154–5
Nissen huts 82
nonagenarian 11
North Ronaldshay 40–1

oatmeal 121
octogenarian 87
oil resources 140
One Countryman To Another
117, 193–4
onions 60
Onslow, Earl of 44–5
Orchard Roundabout 134
Orwin, CS 35
ostriches 96–7
Other People's Countrysides 15
outsider 152
owls 105, 193–4

Page, Robin 183, 208, 213–4
Paraguay 13
Parakeets 138

parsnips 53
pedlars 110
Pen yr Ole Wen 186–7
Phelps, Humphrey 168, 180,
183, 197, 201, 205
pickpockets 79
picnickers 74
pig killing 76
pigs 42, 51, 63, 143, 188
pigeons 147
pills, coloured 41
pollution 123, 136, 137
Ponies, New Forest striped 47
pop festivals 134
'Postman Author' 43
posts, upside-down 76
Powell, Eric F 132
Priestley, JB 137
primroses 84
privies 121
pylons 23, 127

Quarendon, R 52–3
Quinn, Tom 182, 203

rabbits 29, 92, 104
see also myxomatosis
Radnorshire 54
railways 119, 145, 153, 180
rationing 69
rats 103
Rawnsley, Irene 175
Reilly, B 158
roads 115, 130–1, 157
Roberts, Dr Harry 67
Robertson Scott, JW 6–7, 8,
36, 68, 101
roosters 61
rose hips 54
'Rusticus' 183
'Salfario' 9, 19–20

'Scavenger' 183, 218
schoolboy, smelly 153
Selborne Giant 190–1
self-sufficiency 125
Severn Bore 132
Sheehan, John 188
sheep 103, 153
shellfish, souls of 89
Shorthorn typist 117
Silcock, Fred 193
Silent Spring 101, 114
Skokholm 37
skylarks 202
slow-worms 88
smoking 71, 79
Snowdonia 186–7
solar energy 112
Somaliland 11
sonization 25
soya beans 52
spiders 71
splarging 210
sprat seeds 81
Spray, Martin 185
Stanham, Edward 144–5
starlings 140–1
stoats 199
Strength and Stay 48–9
Stuart, Frank S 62
'Student' 9
subsidies 209
summer time 87
swans 177

tabernacles, tin 204–5
Tail Corn 10
tails 98
Tate, Ann 197
Taylor, Bill 182
Taylor, Mrs HB 11
tear gas 60

telephone operators 188
tenors 203
Tesco 205
thatch 62, 122
Thatcher, Margaret 151, 160–1
titmice, value of 39
toads 173
toe sucking 49
tongue, false 57
toothache cure 159
tortoises 192
Town and Country Planning
    Act 69
Toynbee, Prof. Arnold 137
tractors 38, 66, 97, 197
traffic, tourist 118–9
tree planting 41, 76
Trends of Agricultural
    Thinking 22, 25
'Triple Bar' 85–6
turkeys 120
Twain, Mark 71

ultraviolet lamps 103
US servicemen 59

vegetarianism 177, 196

From a 1929 advertisement for Lotus Ltd.

Veltom, John 195
vernacular 28, 54, 105, 107
veterinarians 98
village halls 69
village shops 174
Vince, John 183, 210
violet leaves 97
Viyella 36, 77

walking equipment 172
War, Second World 34–67
war memorials 65
water, subterranean 47
Watt, Hew 156, 157
weather, extreme 91, 151, 179
wells 129
Wells, HG 35
Westminster Notebook 218
Westmorland 107
whaling 77
Wheeler, David 182
'Who prop in these bad days'
    35
Wild Life and Tame 35, 61,
    80, 86, 109, 138, 147, 153,
    169, 173, 177, 181, 189, 192,
    194
Will o' the Wisps 193
Wilson, Colin 152
Wilson, Major John 67
windfarms 212
Winstanley, Lord 151
Winstone, Reece 107
Wiseacre, Solomon 9, 50
woodlice 197
Wood, Wendy 99
Wright, D Macer 134

yew trees 190–1

Zealey, Philip 112

Credits

Acknowledgments

Valerie Porter would like to thank Paul Jackson, the current Editor of *The Countryman*, for giving her access to the archives and for being unfailingly helpful during her researches.